It Happened In Series

IT HAPPENED IN
VERMONT

Mark Bushnell

gpp

Guilford, Connecticut

Copyright © 2009 by Morris Book Publishing, LLC

Project manager: David Legere
Layout: Joanna Beyer
Text design: Nancy Freeborn
Map: Daniel Lloyd © Morris Book Publishing, LLC

Library of Congress Cataloging-in-Publication Data is available on file.

ISBN 978-0-7627-4452-7

Printed in the United States of America

10 9 8 7 6 5 4 3 2 1

To my mother, Marietta, and her fellow librarians everywhere

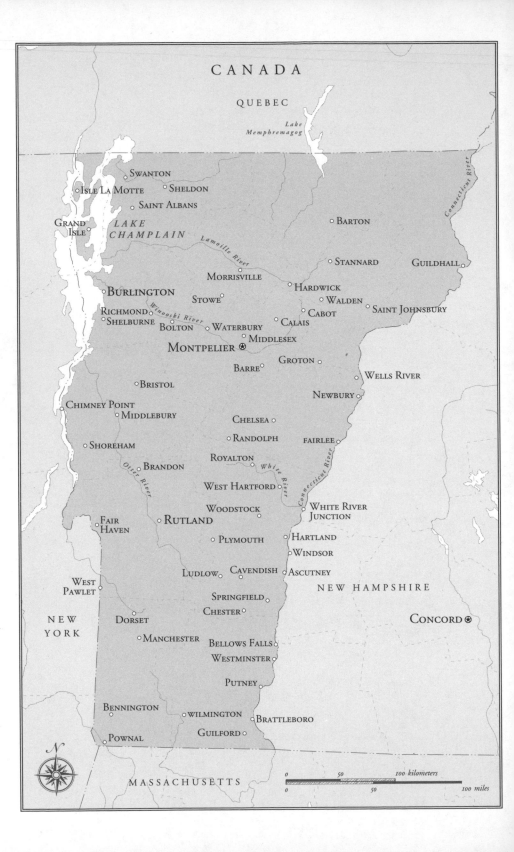

CANADA

QUEBEC

Lake
Memphremagog

Connecticut River

SWANTON

ISLE LA MOTTE
SHELDON

SAINT ALBANS

BARTON

GRAND
ISLE

LAKE
CHAMPLAIN

Lamoille River

STANNARD
GUILDHALL

MORRISVILLE

BURLINGTON
STOWE
HARDWICK

WALDEN

Winooski River
CABOT
SAINT JOHNSBURY

RICHMOND
SHELBURNE
BOLTON
WATERBURY
CALAIS

MONTPELIER ✪
MIDDLESEX

BARRE
GROTON

WELLS RIVER

BRISTOL

NEWBURY

CHIMNEY POINT
MIDDLEBURY

CHELSEA

SHOREHAM
RANDOLPH
FAIRLEE

BRANDON
ROYALTON
White River

Otter River

WEST HARTFORD
Connecticut River

WOODSTOCK
WHITE RIVER
JUNCTION

FAIR
HAVEN
RUTLAND

PLYMOUTH
HARTLAND

WINDSOR

LUDLOW
CAVENDISH
ASCUTNEY

WEST
PAWLET

NEW HAMPSHIRE

SPRINGFIELD

CHESTER

NEW
YORK

DORSET
CONCORD ✪

MANCHESTER

BELLOWS FALLS

WESTMINSTER

PUTNEY

BENNINGTON
WILMINGTON
BRATTLEBORO

POWNAL
GUILFORD

N

0   50   100 kilometers
0   50   100 miles

MASSACHUSETTS

CONTENTS

CONTENTS

INTRODUCTION

Biologists say the edge is where the action is. Where two ecological zones meet—where water meets shore, where forest meets field— that's where things get interesting. Perhaps that explains why Vermont has had such a rich history for such a small place. Though it has been physically remote from the major centers of power—the ones that created European colonies on this continent, then forged a new nation, fought over it during the Civil War, and governed it in the years since—Vermont has felt the tumult.

Vermont is situated on the boundary where nations, colonies, and factions have collided for centuries. The written history of the region begins in the early 1600s with the arrival of the French, as they moved south from what is now Canada. Native Americans, of course, already occupied the area. That overlap sparked Vermont's first conflict recorded in writing.

Then, in the following century, the French found themselves battling, and ultimately losing to, the British, who were moving north. But that did little to settle matters. Vermont was still disputed territory. The surrounding colonies—New York, New Hampshire, and Massachusetts—all laid claim to it. Out of these land squabbles arose a faction of ornery and independent-minded people determined to be free of these disputes. These were the founders of the state of Vermont, the legendarily pugnacious Green Mountain

Boys and the politicians who followed in their wake. They are the forebears of modern Vermonters, though we have toned down the orneriness a bit.

When Vermonters agreed to surrender their autonomy and joined the United States—a decision that still rankles some today—they chose as their state motto "Freedom and Unity." It was an apt choice, the phrase recognizing their independent spirit but also acknowledging that for a civilization to survive it requires neighborly cooperation.

In this book, you'll meet people who helped shape the state, and who were shaped by it. Among them are the unfortunate French soldiers who, during the 1660s, experienced the full force of a Vermont winter; the Vermont congressman who fought for his right to criticize the president, and was jailed for his pains; the farmers and others who suffered through the "Year Without a Summer"; the people of St. Albans who, because of their proximity to Canada, bore the brunt of a startling cross-border attack from Confederates that proved to be the farthest-north battle of the Civil War; and the Vermonters who rejected the advice of out-of-state "experts" and defeated the federal plan to run a highway along the spine of the Green Mountains.

In short, you'll learn that things get interesting when you are living on the edge.

A KILLING WINTER FOR THE FRENCH

1666–1667

SEVERAL DOZEN FRENCHMEN HUDDLED INSIDE a small fort on an island in the middle of Lake Champlain during the winter of 1666, about as far from Western civilization as anyone could have imagined. As they lay awake at night in their frigid cabins and worried about the sickness spreading among them, each must have wondered: "What am I doing here?"

It was a fair question.

The sixty men were the soldiers of Fort Sainte Anne, the southernmost bastion in this part of New France, as the French colonial empire in North America was called. They were expected to menace the Iroquois, who had been challenging French control of the area. At particularly bleak moments, the soldiers must have realized that as New France's first line of attack, they could easily become its first line of defense. They may also have realized that military leaders had little faith this fort would hold. Just north of Fort Sainte Anne, the French had built a series of three more strongholds along the Richelieu River to help block any invasion.

Relations had always been bad between the French and Iroquois. The Iroquois had first met the French in 1609, at the wrong end of Samuel de Champlain's gun. Seeking allies in the fur trade, Champlain had tried to curry favor with the Iroquois' rivals, the Algonquin tribes. He agreed to accompany a war party of Abenaki and Montagnais (tribes in the Algonquin nation) south on the lake that today bears his name and into the territory of the Iroquois. When the anticipated clash occurred, Champlain raised his long arquebus (a predecessor of the musket) and shot dead several Iroquois. This shocking display of violence had the desired effect in the short term. It scared away the Iroquois. Unfortunately for the French, it also sparked nearly a century of intermittent warfare with the Iroquois.

By the 1640s, the Iroquois also had firearms, which they took in trade from English and Dutch allies. After crushing rival tribes, they began following Lake Champlain north and raiding the new French settlements of Trois-Rivieres and Montreal.

In response, the French had begun building forts along the Richelieu. By 1665, three were completed. Then in January 1666, the French colonial governor launched an assault against the Mohawks, one of the six Indian nations that formed the Iroquois. Six hundred soldiers trudged south during what was the harshest winter in decades. They slept exposed to the elements and ran low on food before being ambushed in what is today upstate New York. The survivors retreated north, their hunger growing worse. They failed to find provisions cached on one of the Champlain Islands. Among the losses were sixty men who starved or froze to death on the return march.

That's when French colonial officials ordered the construction of a fort farther south, Fort Sainte Anne. It would be a way station for troops headed south and a defense against Indian attackers heading north. Three hundred men labored during the summer of 1666 to build the rectangular island fort, which measured 144 feet by 96 feet and featured a fifteen-foot palisade fence with a bastion at each corner. Inside the fort were fourteen buildings to house the troops. They were led by Capt. Pierre de St. Paul, Sieur de la Motte, after whom the island would be named.

French authorities put the fort to immediate use. That fall of 1666 they assembled in and around the fort a force of 1,300 men who would attack Mohawk villages to the south. Half the soldiers were crack troops who had just shipped in from France. Their use suggests how seriously the French government took this fight. The other troops were Canadian militia, accompanied by roughly one hundred Hurons and Algonquins.

This expedition into Mohawk territory proved less ill-fated than the previous one, which isn't saying much. The large force approached Mohawk villages, marching to drums, and not surprisingly, found them empty upon their arrival. With no one to fight, the French burned the villages and destroyed the provisions they found. Hundreds of Mohawks are believed to have starved that winter as a result. The French didn't return to the fort unscathed. As canoes capsized during their travels up and down Lake Champlain, they lost eighteen men to the icy waters.

The surviving troops continued back to Canada, except for an unlucky sixty who were ordered to protect Fort Sainte Anne that winter. The writings of one of the men, Francois Dollier de Casson, a Sulpician priest, offer a glimpse of their suffering. Dollier de Casson's job was to minister to the sick and the dying. Upon arriving, he found most of the men suffering from scurvy, which people little understood then. Some believed it was brought on by dampness and was contagious.

The problem, of course, was their diet. The men had subsisted on bread and dried meat. Deprived of fresh fruit and vegetables, they had developed a severe vitamin C deficiency. Victims of scurvy suffered general weakness and joint pain. Their bodies showed bruises from internal bleeding. Their breath turned foul, their gums bled, and their teeth fell out. Untreated, they would die.

As much as disease or death, the men feared dying without a priest to pray for their souls. When Dollier de Casson arrived, La Motte rushed out to greet him. "Welcome! What a pity you did not arrive a little earlier!" La Motte said. "How the two soldiers who have just died longed for you!"

The "death agony," Dollier de Casson reported, "lasted eight days, during which the stench was so great that it reached almost to the center of the fort, although the patients were shut up in their rooms."

The priest witnessed dying men doing what they could to ensure that their comrades took care of them. The sick "set about making elaborate wills, as if they had been very rich, saying 'I give so much to so and so because he helped me in my last illness. . .' Those who saw through the device smiled at the resource of these poor fellows, who did not have a cent in the world."

During his time at Fort Sainte Anne, the priest would attend eleven more deaths.

Like others, Dollier de Casson thought scurvy contagious—what else explained why so many contracted with it at once? He took care to keep himself healthy. As a new arrival who until recently had eaten well, he actually had nothing to worry about for months. When he wasn't working or sleeping, Dollier de Casson would go to the edges of the fort, where the snow had been tramped down, "to take the air and run back and forth, in order to avoid the disease."

Anyone who saw me would have thought me crazy, had
he not known how essential such violent exercise was to

keep off the illness. It was certainly funny to watch me say my breviary [daily prayers] on the run, but I had no other time.

Dollier de Casson had brought with him the prayers the soldiers longed for with their souls. He brought something equally important for their bodies—fresh food. Well connected with the colonial government, Dollier de Casson had secured a shipment of provision. He and the others seemed to understand that this fresher food might help ward off the sickness.

La Motte stored the food in his room. He didn't realize it, but his greatest service to his men was his nightly rationing out of stewed prunes, which are rich in vitamin C. "This was the only way to cure them," Dollier de Casson said astutely, though he added that "the air was so infected at St. Anne [that] not one who stayed recovered." That first winter, half the men died.

The French only maintained the fort for a few years. Skirmishes with the Iroquois had abated, at least temporarily, so they decided they no longer needed the stronghold. Sometime between 1669 and 1671, they abandoned the fort. Soldiers set the fence and buildings on fire so that no others could use the place, and they headed north to civilization.

THE WESTMINSTER MASSACRE

1775

WILLIAM FRENCH WAS DEAD. That much was obvious. How he died was also beyond debate; he'd been shot five times. But the significance of his death remains open to interpretation. To some, French was one of the first martyrs to the cause of American liberty and one of the earliest Revolutionary heroes to come from what is now Vermont. To others, he was merely the victim of a public disturbance that turned violent.

This much is sure: French was shot at about 11:00 p.m. on March 13, 1775, while he and about one hundred other men were occupying the courthouse in Westminster, which the Colony of New York then regarded as part of its Cumberland County. French and the others were trying to keep the court from opening its session. The men camped in the courthouse were mostly farmers who feared losing their lands. Money was in short supply, so it was difficult to pay off debts. Several days earlier, a delegation of forty men from Rockingham had approached Judge Thomas Chandler, who ran the local court, asking to delay the court session until after the harvest, so they could meet their debts. The judge said he would consider the request, though he had to open the court to try a murder case.

But many didn't trust Judge Chandler to keep his word. So on March 13, a crowd marched along muddy roads from Rockingham to occupy the blocky, two-story building with a gambrel roof, which they found empty. The building was one of the newest structures in a town still being settled. Downstairs, the courthouse contained a wide hallway. On one side was a pair of cells. On the other stood a kitchen for the jailer and a room for lawyers and litigants. Upstairs was the still unfinished courtroom.

Hearing of the protest, Sheriff William Paterson of Hinsdale (now the town of Vernon) gathered a posse of about twenty-five men in Brattleboro and marched them north. As they came, others joined. Paterson had armed his men with wooden staves. But some who joined along the route carried muskets. By the time the posse reached Westminster, it numbered about fifty.

Arriving to find the courthouse occupied, Paterson read aloud a proclamation from King George III, a standard document calling for the court session to begin. He gave the protesters fifteen minutes to leave the building. The two sides exchanged insults, but no one left the courthouse. Perhaps hoping to avoid violence, Paterson withdrew his men to the comforts of the nearby Norton's tavern to wait.

At this point—it was about 7:00 p.m.—Judge Chandler entered the courthouse and tried to talk the protesters into leaving. He promised to hear the complaints in court, but they must let it start, he said. The protesters were unmoved, so Chandler left.

About four hours later, they learned that the "sheriff and his men were coming, with courage reinforced by potations of flip and fiery rum," according to Rowland Robinson in his 1892 history *Vermont: A Study of Independence*.

Perhaps they meant to sneak up on the protesters as they slept, but they were too large and perhaps too inebriated a group to move quietly. Instead of stealth, Paterson chose a more direct approach, climbing the stairs and demanding to be let in.

What happened next is unclear. Paterson later said he was clubbed by sentries and pushed down the stairs. Those inside the courthouse claimed Paterson had been so drunk he had fallen down the stairs on his own.

Whatever occurred, someone ordered the posse to fire its guns into the courthouse. Posse members later said they fired three warning shots, and the protesters fired back. Only then did Paterson's men shoot to kill. The protesters said they had been armed only with clubs.

Ten protesters were hit by musket balls. The posse stormed the courthouse. As protesters fled, the posse grabbed nine or ten men and locked them in the cells. Among those seized was the mortally wounded William French, whom, according to one account, "they dragged as one would a dog, and would mock at [him] as he lay gasping."

Some claimed French, who was twenty-one, was left untended, but another version of the story says two doctors were called. Either way, he was beyond saving. A second protester, Daniel Houghton of Dummerston, would die more than a week after French. But his death is largely forgotten, because by that time work was already under way to turn French into a martyr—the "proto-martyr" of the Revolution, in one writer's opinion.

Ethan Allen and the Green Mountain Boys pounced on the incident for political advantage. Their power base was in southwestern Vermont, around Bennington, and they had long clashed with settlers in the Brattleboro area. The conflict was over who each faction believed had the right to grant land charters. Allen and his followers owed their land to grants issued by the colony of New Hampshire, whereas people around Brattleboro got their land from New York. But now New York, in exerting its authority to operate a court in the region, had caused the death of a local man.

Allen dispatched about forty men to Brattleboro to defend opponents of Yorker rule. The "Westminster Massacre," as it was soon dubbed, helped galvanize some Brattleboro-area residents to oppose New York. The incident unnerved New York's acting governor, Cadwallader Colden, who wrote British general Thomas Gage, asking for help ensuring that the court could be opened. But Gage could offer no assistance. Things were getting hot in Boston.

The Westminster court opened the next day in what was still nominally Cumberland County, New York. The judges sat nervously while outside local militiamen, who opposed British and New York authority, began to gather in town. Units from New Hampshire and Massachusetts soon joined them. Sensing danger, members of Paterson's posse began to slip away. The judges postponed the murder trial, which had previously been deemed too important to delay, and began asking questions about what had happened the previous night. They adjourned shortly after 3:00 p.m. It would be the last act of outside authority in what is today Vermont.

THE ROAD FROM
NOWHERE TO NOWHERE

1776

IT WAS AN URGENT MILITARY RESUPPLY MISSION. With hundreds of troops behind enemy lines and hostile forces pursuing them, the commanding general approved a plan to get much-needed reinforcements and materiel to them.

With none of the split-second timing such a mission implies today, this operation moved at its own eighteenth-century pace. The year was 1776 and the commander was General George Washington. The plan would take months to implement because it involved carving a new road, a shortcut, through more than ninety miles of wilderness in what today is Vermont.

The situation was this: The Continental Army had tried—and spectacularly failed—to conquer British-held Canada. Washington and others had believed that once the invasion force made its presence felt, Canadians would rise up against their British oppressors. But it didn't happen that way.

The Continental Army had managed to take Montreal. But an assault on Quebec City proved a debacle in which sixty Americans died and four hundred were captured. The remaining five hundred troops withdrew and hunkered down, still within Quebec, awaiting reinforcements.

The nearest relief was at Fort Number Four in Charlestown, N.H. The fastest route from the fort to Quebec was by water, following rivers and creeks to Crown Point, then north up Lake Champlain. It was a journey of about 165 miles.

Colonel Jacob Bayley saw a better way. He wrote Washington, urging him to have a road cut from Wells River northwest to St. Johns, Quebec. Surveyors had found good terrain for such a road, which would cover only ninety-two miles, seventy-three miles shorter than the water route.

Washington received Bayley's report in April 1776, and he loved the idea. "The Time of Congress is so taken up with many objects of Consequence, that it is impossible for them to attend to every Thing," Washington responded the same day. With Congress busy, he made the decision himself: "[I]t is my opinion and desire, that you set about the Road you propose as soon as possible." The general could not spare any soldiers to help with construction, so he instructed Bayley to hire local workers. "I will provide for the expense," he promised, "which you will be careful in making as light as possible."

Bayley hired 110 men, paying them $10 a month, plus food and a half pint of rum a day. The men cut a road wide enough for a wagon to pass. In wet spots, they used corduroy construction, laying trees across the road and covering them with dirt—a bumpy ride, but better than a quagmire. After six weeks, the road extended the roughly twenty miles from Wells River to Peacham, and proceeded six miles past it.

Then Bayley received a startling letter from Washington. "[O]ur Army in Canada, since their retreat from Quebec[,] has met with further Misfortunes," he informed Bayley. The army might have to retreat out of Canada, or perhaps had already done so, Washington reported.

The thought that remnants of his invasion force might be heading south apparently gave Washington an idea that, oddly, he hadn't seriously considered before: British soldiers might also use the new road to invade south. If completed, it would link to an existing road system that led to Boston. Washington realized the road would afford the British "an easy Pass to make Incursions into our Colonies to commit Depredations."

He warned Bayley that the "Change which has taken Place in our Affairs in that Quarter may render now what was extremely right to be done some Thing very inexpedient and unadvisable."

Despite the obvious risk that a cross-border road would aid an invasion force heading either direction, Washington did something curious. He left it to Bayley to decide whether to stop construction.

Not surprisingly, Bayley erred on the side of caution and shut down the project. Possibly, he had already done so before receiving Washington's letter, having heard of the Continental Army's condition from deserters heading south. With the road not yet reaching Quebec, the retreating army followed the traditional water route south to Fort Ticonderoga in New York and Mount Independence in Vermont.

Despite Washington's promises, Congress never repaid Bayley the money he had spent on the endeavor.

Two years later, a road north again seemed advisable. The Continental Army was considering another invasion of Canada. This time General Moses Hazen was given orders to complete the project. Bayley and Hazen, whose names are forever attached in the name of the route, the Bayley-Hazen Military Road, were acquainted. Bayley was good friends with Hazen's brother, John, and both held substantial land grants in the Newbury area.

Hazen pushed the work forward cautiously, building blockhouses every few miles along the route and fortifying their perimeters.

The men built blockhouses in Cabot and Walden and one at Caspian Lake. Hazen grew skittish, feeling that his left flank was vulnerable. He halted road construction once it reached a notch in the mountains of Westfield that today bears his name. The road that started in Newbury petered out after fifty-seven miles.

Washington's belated concerns about the road being useful to the British proved justified. In fact, some historians suggest that the British got more use out of the road than the Americans. The British used the road to lead small attacks on colonial forces stationed nearby. At one point, a small British contingent even tried to capture Bayley, who was living in Newbury. The general, however, had been warned and evaded capture.

For all the debate over the advisability of building the road, and for all the actual labor put into it, the Bayley-Hazen Military Road never proved an important factor in the war. Indeed, some call it "the road from nowhere to nowhere."

THE ROYALTON RAID

1780

THEY HAD NO WARNING, unless you count the dog that barked at something in the woods the day before. Probably wolves, his master had figured.

So, when the attack came before daybreak on October 16, 1780, the people of Royalton were caught off guard. A band of roughly three hundred Indians rampaged through the widely spread homesteads that made up the town. As they went, the Indians ransacked and burned houses and farm buildings, slaughtered livestock, took twenty-six prisoners, and killed two male settlers.

Directing the Indians, most of them Caughnawaga Mohawks, was a handful of British soldiers, seven in all. This was the third and most violent raid that summer and fall against a settlement in the area. Barnard and Bethel had been hit in August and September, respectively.

Now it was Royalton's turn to suffer.

Why Royalton? There are any number of answers. First, it was one of the outposts that marked the northwest corner of New

England. The line of settlement ran across Vermont roughly from current-day Addison County to Newbury on the Connecticut River. Forts, located at places such as Pittsford, Bethel, Barnard, and Royalton, protected settlers from invasion forces coming south. Between colonists and the British was a wide swath of land inhabited by Native Americans, whom colonists hoped would serve as a buffer.

So, the attack might have been purely strategic—a probe to test defenses in case the British force in Canada decided to invade via Vermont. Or, perhaps it was more personal.

One theory holds that the attack was payback, part of a tit-for-tat battle between Britain and its rebellious colonies. This particular feud had started with Indian raids—like this one, engineered by the British—in which women and children were killed. General George Washington responded by issuing an order, offering a major's commission and pay to any American soldier who slipped into Canada and killed a British general. Killing a colonel would earn the assassin a captain's commission.

Benjamin Whitcomb, a veteran army scout of high regard, took Washington up on his offer. He crossed stealthily into Canada in 1776 and shot dead a British general as he rode by. Getting out of Canada proved harder than getting in. With British troops and Indian scouts in pursuit, Whitcomb made his way through the wilderness of Quebec and Vermont to Royalton, where residents took him in. Thus, this theory goes, the attack was in response to what the British regarded as cold-blooded murder.

Royalton, however, was not the initial target of the raid. Lieutenant Richard Houghton of the British Indian Detachment and his men had orders to travel down Lake Champlain and cut across the state on the Winooski and other rivers. Their destination was to be Newbury, another key fort and where they hoped to find Whitcomb, who was attached to the unit stationed there.

But, as we know, they changed their minds. Somehow Vermont militia got wind of their plans. One version of the story has it that Houghton mentioned his destination to a man the attackers met near what today is Montpelier. He mistook the man for a Loyalist. In reality, he was an American scout.

Or perhaps less dramatically, the truth is that in those sparsely settled times, it was hard to sneak a group of three hundred men unnoticed down one of the state's main thoroughfares. Once spotted, it took little guesswork to figure out that they planned to attack one of the communities upstream.

At some point, Houghton realized that the American militia would be waiting for him in Newbury. Four years earlier, when they had feared an attack, the militia had rallied three hundred to four hundred men, who built breastworks and a blockhouse to protect Newbury. Perhaps taking on Newbury would be too fair a fight.

So Houghton changed course, ordering his men over the hills to Chelsea, down the First Branch of the White River, which runs through Tunbridge, and then into Royalton.

After the devastating raid, the attackers retreated quickly through Randolph and Brookfield, where they captured a man named Zadock Steele, who would later write of his time as a captive.

From Steele, we learn of the odd mix of cruelty and kindness captives experienced as they were marched to Canada. Two of the captives were killed by the Indians, apparently in revenge for their earlier involvement in the murder of some Indians. The Indians also threatened to kill any captive who fell behind on the march. But these threats stopped as soon as it was clear the pursuing militiamen had lost their trail. Then, the Indians could be quite humane. If a captive stopped to eat berries along the hike, the Indians would assume he was hungry and offer him food.

It is not surprising that Native Americans felt conflicted about their captives. The allegiances of the various tribes had been shifting for years. This "fickleness," as the Americans called it, frustrated both sides in the conflict. British general Guy Carleton complained that the Indians only supported whichever side seemed stronger. Indeed, the Caughnawagas told American settlers that they helped the British only because the British had threatened to destroy them otherwise. In short, they were keeping their options open during tumultuous times.

Marching north, the captives faced an uncertain future. Captives before them had met various fates. Some had been murdered in retaliation for the killing of warriors by whites. Others had been washed in a river to rid them of their "whiteness" and then adopted into Indian families that had lost a warrior. Sometimes the adoption was complete and mutual. When some captives were ransomed, they refused to return home, finding Native American life preferable to the one from which they had been torn.

The captives of the Royalton raid faced no such quandary. They were handed over to British authorities, who jailed them and kept them cold and hungry. One died while in jail. Steele recalls the Indians as far kinder captors than the British. The remaining prisoners were ransomed or exchanged within two years, and all opted to return to America, many of them settling again in Vermont.

So perhaps it is understandable that British general Frederick Haldimand saw little hope of converting Vermont settlers into loyal subjects. To him, these people "are a profligate Banditti, and are now become desperate." He ordered an end to Indian raids into Vermont, figuring they might only serve to turn undecided settlers into rebels. The Royalton Raid, he apparently thought, had been a mistake.

THE COW WARS

1782

SOUTHEASTERN VERMONT WAS IN TURMOIL. The region was on the verge of warfare. Many settlers in the area owed their land grants and, therefore, their allegiance to the former colony of New York. As such, these "Yorkers" bristled at efforts by the so-called government of Vermont to exert power over them.

Into this mess, one day in August 1782, walked Sheriff Barzilla Rice. He had been ordered by the territorial government of Vermont to travel to the town of Guilford, near Brattleboro, to seize a cow that belonged to a Yorker who had refused to be drafted into the Vermont militia. The cow was to be confiscated because it was worth the equivalent of the fine Vermont levied against draft dodgers.

A crowd of Yorkers gathered and scared away Rice—an act of defiance that was just one incident in what has become known in Vermont history as the "Cow Wars."

The conflict actually began three years earlier over the sovereignty question when the so-called Arlington Junta, which was essentially the government of Vermont, ordered Revolutionary

War hero Ethan Allen into the area to bring the populace to heel. The order came from Thomas Chittenden, who eventually went on to become the state of Vermont's first governor: "You are hereby commanded, in the name of the freemen of Vermont, to engage one hundred able bodied effective men . . . " and march them into southeastern Vermont. "Hereof you may not fail," wrote Chittenden.

Allen quickly rounded up one hundred volunteers and started the thirty-mile journey across the southern end of the state toward Guilford. Soon others joined them, armed with old rifles and swords. As they neared Brattleboro, Allen's force totaled nearly 250. It was, one historian wrote, something of a reunion of the Green Mountain Boys, who together had seized Fort Ticonderoga four years earlier. News of the column's approach frightened the Yorkers, who sent an urgent message to New York governor George Clinton, beseeching him for aid: "otherwise our Persons and Property must be at the disposal of Ethan Allin which is more to be dreaded than Death with all its Terrors."

Clinton refused to help.

Despite Yorkers' fears, no one was killed or seriously injured when Allen and his men swept through the area. They arrested thirty leaders of the revolt and delivered them to the town of Westminster for trial. To Allen's consternation, the judge merely issued the Yorkers small fines and rebuked them for disobeying the government. And then Chittenden pardoned all who had revolted. Showing that he had the power to have the men arrested and hauled into a Vermont court would be enough to settle the issue of sovereignty, Chittenden apparently believed. But dissent in the region continued. And it was particularly obvious in Guilford, which for a time had two town governments and two town meetings, one loyal to Vermont, the other to New York.

Soon the unfortunate Sheriff Rice was dispatched to fetch the cow. When a mob chased him off, Chittenden called out the militia a second time. To prevent any repeat of such mob action, the Vermont Assembly banned all future gatherings of more than five people who intended to hinder the execution of the law. Yorkers could still protest the confiscation of cows, but not en masse. Vermont's leaders were willing to limit individual freedoms while the state itself was fighting for freedom from New York.

On September 10, Allen arrived with about 250 men. The town seemed peaceful at first, but suddenly Allen's force was ambushed by about fifty armed Yorkers. Upon hearing the first shots, Allen's militiamen broke for the rear. None of them had been killed or even wounded. The firing had apparently been merely warning shots.

Allen rallied his troops and led his column back to the ambush site. There, according to one Yorker witness, Allen shouted out a threat: "I, Ethan Allen, do declare that I will give no quarter to the man, woman or child who shall oppose me and unless the inhabitants of Guilford peacefully submit to the authority of Vermont, I swear that I will lay it as desolate as Sodom and Gomorrah, by God."

That did the trick. The Yorkers scattered. Allen and his troops marched on unmolested and arrested twenty leaders of the revolt, who were again packed off to Westminster for trial. There, Allen at first tried to win them over to Vermont's side, arguing that it was in their financial self-interest. If Vermonters "would be united," he told them, "they might make independent fortunes, while the 13 united states were quarreling among themselves and becoming bankrupts."

Most of the Yorkers came around to accepting Vermont's sovereignty. They were fined and released. Four, however, refused to acknowledge Vermont's control of the region or admit any wrongdoing. For this, the court banished them and ordered their property seized.

Tensions continued. Yorkers, at the urging of Governor Clinton, kidnapped a former Vermont lieutenant governor, Benjamin Carpenter. Vermont responded by arresting a few Yorkers. Carpenter was released after promising to ask the Vermont Assembly to release its Yorker prisoners, but the Assembly refused to do so.

After a fight between Vermonters and Yorkers at a Brattleboro inn, the Vermont militia—this time under the command of General Samuel Fletcher—was again dispatched to quell the rebels. With Vermont militiamen approaching, one hundred Yorkers vowed to fight to the death. They fired on the advancing troops, mortally wounding one of them, then fled south. The Yorkers dispersed as the militia advanced, some fleeing across the Massachusetts line.

Ethan Allen arrived two days later with reinforcements. He declared martial law in Brattleboro, stationed a regiment in Guilford, and ordered any straggling Yorkers arrested. Vermont was tired of dissenters. When Yorkers petitioned the Vermont Assembly for pardons, their messenger was arrested.

Voters at Guilford's town meeting—the one loyal to Vermont, that is—offered to forgive anyone who swore allegiance to Vermont. Many Yorkers took the oath. The back of the rebel uprising was finally broken. New York's governor would continue to oppose Vermont's legitimacy for another half dozen years, but he would have to do so without any organized support from within Vermont.

THE VISIT OF TWO FOUNDERS

1791

THE MEN WERE TRAVELING INCOGNITO. They wanted to get away from the madding crowd and the crushing pressures of their work. Though this vacation was for pleasure, they couldn't help mixing in a little business along the way—they were compulsively active people. And they were among the most famous visitors ever to set foot in Vermont.

On May 31, 1791, a small boat set sail across Lake Champlain, carrying Thomas Jefferson and James Madison from the New York side to the Vermont shore. They were excited by the prospect of exploring what was then a wild and remote region of the new country. Just three months earlier, in fact, Jefferson, as secretary of state, had officially attested to Vermont's entering the union. Madison, then an influential member of Congress, seems to have been equally interested in this new state that was joining the original thirteen.

They spent their first night in Vermont at an inn at Chimney Point. They had hoped to get farther up the lake, but had run into foul weather and been forced to find shelter. Their brief cruise up the lake and their stay at the Chimney Point Tavern gave the men a chance to observe the people and animals of this strange place.

Madison jotted in his notes that Vermonters led simple lives. "Their living [is] extremely plain and economical, particularly in the table and ordinary dress," he wrote. "Their expense is chiefly on their houses, which are of wood and make a good figure [outside], but are very scantily furnished within."

Vermont held great potential in Jefferson's eyes. To him, the state could be a new Virginia, but without the deep-rooted slave system and aristocracy. It could be a place where ordinary farmers could own land and make a living. His beliefs had been reaffirmed when he crossed the slender section of lake separating New York and Vermont. Whereas New Yorkers were tenant farmers, Vermonters owned their own farms, he noted.

Jefferson, an accomplished naturalist, was also fascinated by the presence around the inn of countless red squirrels of a species he had never before encountered. "We have met with a small red squirrel, of the color of our fox squirrel with a black stripe on each side," he wrote. The squirrels were "in such abundance, on Lake Champlain particularly . . . that twenty odd were killed at the house we lodged in . . . without going ten steps from the door."

After spending the night at the inn (today a state historic site), the men continued sailing north. Facing a stiff north wind and already behind schedule, they scrapped plans to sail all the way to the Canadian border and then cross the Green Mountains. Instead, they would head to Saratoga, N.Y., scene of the great American victory during the recent Revolution, then travel by land to Bennington.

Despite their best efforts to travel unnoticed, news of their plans beat them to Bennington. Moses Robinson, former governor and then a U.S. senator, learned they were in town, And he wouldn't hear of Thomas Jefferson and James Madison staying at the local tavern.

He invited them to dine and lodge at his home. They accepted the invitation and that afternoon ate with a group of Vermont political leaders.

Upon arriving, Jefferson had stood enthralled by an immense balsam poplar in Robinson's yard. Jefferson was that sort of guy, and this was a new world to him. But it was a different sort of tree he spoke of over dinner. Jefferson had noted the abundant maple trees that blanketed Vermont and thought they could benefit the nation. He envisioned a maple sugar industry that would eliminate the nation's dependence on foreign sugar, then the country's largest import.

The *Vermont Gazette* trumpeted the news of Jefferson's plans to have a Dutch company set up a maple operation in the state. "Refineries are about [to be] established by some wealthy foreigners resident in the Union," the paper reported. The Dutch firm's operation did indeed open, but soon failed. Vermonters, however, had gotten the message that their maple trees were valuable.

Jefferson and the other guests no doubt also discussed politics. At the dinner, Madison and Jefferson apparently learned the distressing news that the British had built an armed blockhouse on North Hero, a Vermont island just south of the Canadian border, and that a British warship was harassing shipping on the lake.

The men wanted to leave the next morning, but it was a Sunday and Vermont had strict blue laws prohibiting travel on the Sabbath. So instead they accompanied Robinson to the town's Congregational meetinghouse, where they received a cold reception from the minister, Job Swift, who viewed them as godless slave owners.

Despite Swift's iciness, the two men no doubt saw the promise of this new state. Perhaps the future presidents discussed Vermont's potential as they rose before dawn the next morning and rode toward home.

THE TRIAL OF MATTHEW LYON

1799

MATTHEW LYON WAS A MARKED MAN. During his brief but tempestuous career in national politics, he had made loads of enemies. Now, in October 1798, they seemed to have him cornered. Word of the trouble he was about to face came on October 5, when a deputy served him with an arrest warrant. The charge: sedition against the United States.

It was a severe form of political payback. Lyon was an ardent Jeffersonian Democrat and an outspoken critic of the Federalist Party, which dominated Congress and held the White House, and these were harsh political times. The nation was girding for possible war with France, and the Federalists would brook no dissent. That's why they had just passed the Alien and Sedition Acts, which created a whole raft of new punishable offenses, among them, making "false, scandalous, and malicious" comments about federal officials. The new law was aimed at the Federalists' staunchest opponents, people like Lyon.

The indictment of Lyon, the first person charged under the statute, demonstrated the risks of dissent during the early days of the Republic. Looking at how the case played out shows how political attacks against the administration were distorted and treated as threats to the Republic itself.

Lyon's arrest seems to have been carefully timed. As a member of Congress, he had enjoyed immunity from arrest. But his term had expired and, with it, so had his immunity. He had returned to Vermont to drum up support to return to office.

Unbeknownst to Lyon, a federal circuit court had convened in Rutland, where a grand jury investigated whether Lyon had violated the acts. The jury, presided over by both a U.S. and Vermont Supreme Court justice, handed down three indictments, each related to the publishing of anti-Federalist letters in newspapers.

Riding the fifteen miles from Fair Haven to Rutland to turn himself in, Lyon must have pondered his chances of beating the charges. Any hope he had mustered probably dissolved when he entered the courtroom. Looking at the jury, he saw no acquaintances, no sympathetic faces. Worse, when he learned of the hometowns of the jury members, he feared the panel had been packed with men from Federalist strongholds.

Lyon had no lawyer and none was provided for him. He sent a messenger to Bennington, looking for a lawyer from that strongly Jeffersonian community to represent him. U.S. Supreme Court associate justice William Paterson told Lyon he had the right to postpone the trial until the court met the following May. But that hearing would be in Windsor. Aware that Windsor was crawling with Federalists, Lyon decided to take his chances in Rutland.

When the trial opened two days later, Lyon still had no lawyer. None could make it in time for the hearing. He chose to represent himself. Israel Smith, chief justice of the Vermont Supreme Court, who happened to be watching the proceedings, agreed to assist Lyon, even though Lyon had defeated him in the congressional election two years earlier.

The district attorney began the trial by showing the jury a letter Lyon had written to the *Vermont Journal,* a Federalist newspaper in Windsor. It seems to have been the most damning piece of evidence against Lyon.

In the letter, Lyon rebuked President John Adams and his administration for violating the public trust. Lyon wrote:

> [W]henever I shall, on the part of the executive, see every consideration of the public welfare swallowed up by a continual grasp for power; in an unbounded thirst for ridiculous pomp, foolish adulation, and selfish avarice; when I shall behold men of real merit daily turned out of office, for no other cause but independency of sentiment; . . . and men of meanness preferred for the ease with which they take up and advocate opinions . . . when I shall see the sacred name of religion employed as a state engine to make mankind hate and persecute one another, I shall not be their humble advocate.

The problem for the prosecution was that Lyon had written the letter on June 20 and it bore a July 7 postmark, which was a week before the Alien and Sedition Acts became law. But the letter had not been published until July 31. Perhaps it is no coincidence that the newspaper that had held the letter until after the acts were passed was pro-Federalist.

The second and third charges involved Lyon's publishing of a letter by Joel Barlow, an American expatriate living in France. Barlow, who was pro-French, criticized the United States' actions toward France, singling out a "bullying speech" by Adams and the "stupid" response from the Senate.

In his defense, Lyon challenged the constitutionality of the Alien and Sedition Acts, a question that Paterson said was outside the scope of this court. Lyon then argued that he lacked the "bad intent" required for conviction under the acts. Finally, he argued that he couldn't be convicted because what he had written had been true.

To prove his last point, Lyon asked Paterson, who had dined with President Adams, whether he had noticed any "ridiculous pomp and parade." The judge said he had seen no excessive formality. Then Lyon asked whether he had witnessed "more pomp and servants there than at the tavern at Rutland" where Paterson was lodging.

"The judge," the *Aurora,* a Jeffersonian newspaper in Philadelphia, wrote, "conscious that there was some difference between table at Braintree (Adams' home), and the humble fare of a country tavern, with the privileges of half a bed, made no reply, but smoked a cigar."

The jury took an hour to convict Lyon. Judge Paterson, ignoring Lyon's claims of poverty, fined him $1,000, and ordered him jailed for four months. Lyon was shocked. He'd expected the fine, but not one quite so stiff. And he never thought he'd be imprisoned. Lyon was dragged off to a cold cell in Vergennes, from which wrote a widely published letter complaining about prison conditions.

That, the Federalists must have thought, was the end of Lyon. But his name stayed on the ballot and his newfound celebrity as a political martyr helped make him a folk hero and win him re-election. When he left jail, Lyon rode back to the capital in Philadelphia. People in towns along the way lined the road to watch him pass.

THE SLAVE TRIAL

1802

WHEN WINDSOR VOTERS GATHERED for town meeting in 1800, they debated one of the strangest articles ever placed on a Vermont agenda. After dispensing with the usual election of a moderator, a town clerk, selectmen, and other town officers, they launched into the controversial subject.

Article No. 3 asked them to decide "what measures the Town will take respecting a certain Negro woman by the name of Dinah . . . ." In case there was any ambiguity who Dinah was, the article explained that she had been "purchased and brought into this State about Seventeen years past by Stephen Jacob, Esq."

Dinah was a slave, or at least she had been. Now that she was sick and poor, someone had to pay for her care. The question was who. In those days, towns were responsible for caring for the indigent who had no other place to turn. But Dinah did have a place to go, the selectmen argued. Jacob, as a prominent community member and Dinah's keeper, had a legal and moral responsibility to care for her, they figured. Besides, he could afford to. Jacob, a trained lawyer, saw the case differently. He had no intention of footing the bill alone. He believed that Dinah was the town's responsibility. As a Windsor taxpayer, he owed only his fair share of the burden.

Nothing got resolved that late winter day in 1800. The dispute would continue another two and a half years before reaching the Vermont Supreme Court. When the court gathered in August 1802, only two justices heard the case of Selectmen of Windsor vs. Stephen Jacob, Esquire. The third judge recused himself, citing conflict of interest. If ever there was a case for recusal, this was it. Stephen Jacob was not only the defendant but also a justice on the Supreme Court. In fact, until the previous year he had been chief justice.

Despite Jacob's high position, and the judges' familiarity with him, the lawyer for Windsor refused to soften his view of Jacob's actions. Jacob had purchased Dinah in 1783 and brought her to Windsor. "[S]he continued to live with and serve him as a slave until some time in the year 1800," the lawyer said, "when she became infirm, sick, and blind, and in this condition was discarded by the defendant, and became a public charge. . . ."

To bolster the town's case, Windsor's lawyer presented a bill of sale to prove that Jacob had indeed purchased Dinah. The action brought a quick objection from one of Jacob's lawyers—perhaps fearing the admonition that lawyers representing themselves have "a fool for a client," Jacob had hired two. The lawyer, Charles Marsh, made what was the main argument in Jacob's defense. Dinah was not Jacob's responsibility because he never owned her in Vermont. How could he have? Marsh asked. Hadn't the state banned slavery in its constitution in 1777?

"The bill of sale is void by our constitution," Marsh said. Dinah had been a free woman since she had moved to Vermont in 1783, he contended.

Jonathan Hatch Hubbard, one of Windsor's lawyers, responded that even if Dinah could not have legally been Jacob's slave, she had been so in everything but name. In her years working for him, "[s]he may be presumed to have earned for the master sufficient to maintain her in the decrepitude of old age," Hubbard said. Furthermore, "there is a moral obligation upon the master to support her when incapable of labor."

Hubbard attacked the argument that Dinah had been made free simply by moving to Vermont. Weren't escaping slaves who reached Vermont still subject to the national runaway slave laws? he asked. Marsh tried to switch the subject from a discussion of principles to a discussion of facts. It is true, he said, that Dinah had worked for several years for the Jacob family. "[T]here can be but little doubt, from the excellent character and disposition of her master," said Marsh, trying to bolster Jacob's character, "[that] she would have so continued until this time in sickness and in health." That is, had it not been for some other Windsor residents. "[D]iscovering that she was an excellent servant, and wishing to profit themselves of her labours," Marsh said, "[they] inveigled her from her master's family and service by the siren songs of liberty and equality."

Now Marsh deflected the criticism of Jacob and said it was these unnamed Windsor residents, and by extension the selectmen, who were acting callously. "She spent the vigour of her life with these people, and wasted her strength in their service; and now [that] she is blind, paralytic, and incapable of labour, they aim by this suit to compel the defendant solely to maintain her."

Jacob, "as an inhabitant of the State, in obedience to the constitution," renounced any right to own her as a slave. Now that he had been "deprived of her labours," Marsh asked, was it fair to demand that Jacob pay for Dinah's care?

Evidently, it was not. The court sided with Jacob. In ruling, the judge said that the Vermont Constitution's ban on slavery was the relevant issue here, because Jacob had become a resident of the state. The moment her master moved to Vermont, Dinah became free. And since Dinah was no longer a slave, Jacob was no more liable to support her than was any other Windsor resident, the court ruled.

Even after the case was resolved, Windsor's selectmen still bristled at the need to pay for Dinah's care. Records show that in 1806 and 1807, the selectmen tried to warn her out of town, a legal procedure at the time for informing a poor person that the town would not pay for their care.

The town might have seemed indifferent to Dinah's plight, but it continued to pay her bills. Records show the town paying $4 to one resident for briefly boarding her and $20 to another for a longer stay. The documents also note her decline. One entry reads: "Paid Nahum Trask for attending Judge Jacob's Dinah in her last sickness—$14.00." The last notation says, "Paid Barnard Norton—making coffin and tolling bell for Judge Jacob's Dinah—$3.00. Pd. Josiah Hawley, digging grave, $1.50." The court might have ruled otherwise, but in Windsor at least, the former slave remained "Judge Jacob's Dinah."

THE *BLACK SNAKE* AFFAIR

1808

THE *BLACK SNAKE* WAS MORE THAN JUST A BOAT. It was also a symbol, a symbol that divided Vermonters. Many, a majority perhaps, supported the actions of the *Black Snake*'s crew. Others thought the sailors were little more than thieving pirates.

That's because the *Black Snake* was no ordinary sailboat. It was, in fact, a smuggling boat, the most famous ever on Lake Champlain. The *Black Snake*'s success drew the attention of federal authorities, who hunted the boat, hoping to make an example of the famed craft. Ultimately, when the *Black Snake* was cornered, it would lash out and draw blood in an episode that would mark its end.

The career of the *Black Snake* began and ended in 1808. That's the year President Thomas Jefferson declared a ban on trade with British-controlled Canada. The embargo was meant to teach Great Britain a lesson. Instead it taught many Vermonters to disobey their government. Given the state's geography, Vermont relied heavily on trade with Canada. The embargo took food out of people's mouths.

But, in imposing the trade ban, Jefferson was thinking of international issues, not local ones. Britain was at war with France and took it as a sign of hostility that the United States still traded with France. In fairness, the United States still traded with Britain, too. But British leaders had never quite gotten over losing their former colonies and regarded Americans as disloyal. As a result, Britain began seizing American merchant ships, in violation of international law, and sometimes pressing sailors from those ships into service, claiming that they were really British deserters. When a British frigate fired on an American warship, killing three sailors, Jefferson declared the embargo.

Vermonters reacted in anger when they learned of the ban in January 1808, but practiced restraint because they quickly found ways to circumvent it. The act outlawed trade using "ships and vessels." Surely that didn't prevent trade involving lumber rafts or goods carried overland, Vermonters figured.

Congress spotted the loophole almost as quickly as Vermonters had and moved to close it. Federal Collector of Customs Jabez Penniman, a Jefferson appointee in Vermont, learned of the tightened embargo on April 1. If Vermonters who relied on trade were angered by the original restrictions, he knew that they would explode when they learned that all exports north were now banned. Penniman understood the minds of Vermont merchants. After all, he was married to Fanny Allen, widow of Ethan Allen, whose family had invested heavily in Canadian trade. Penniman immediately wrote to the federal government, saying he needed men to enforce the embargo.

Jefferson responded by declaring that "sundry persons are . . . confederating on Lake Champlain and the country thereto adjacent, for the purpose of forming insurrections against the authority of the laws of the United States." As such, Jefferson announced, Penniman and other authorities could defend the embargo by force if necessary.

Penniman hired and armed some local men, but Governor Israel Smith quickly replaced them with a more organized group, the Franklin County brigade of the state militia. Smith soon began to doubt the loyalty of these men, however, since they were from the border area, and presumably knew some of the smugglers. Some militia members might have been smugglers themselves. The governor decided to replace the Franklin County brigade with 150 militiamen from Rutland County, apparently because they lived far from the border.

Despite the efforts of Penniman and the militiamen, smuggling continued unabated. Smugglers paddled and sailed their boats into Missisquoi Bay at the north end of Lake Champlain and into Canada. Others drove herds of animals across the border.

The smugglers weren't simply a group of unpatriotic profiteers. The embargo had choked exports from northern New England, leaving the region suddenly awash in raw materials. To unload this surplus of such commodities as potash (ashes used by soap- and glassmaking operations), lumber, cattle, and swine, northern New Englanders looked for ways to continue trade with Canada.

Some Vermonters went to great lengths to obey the letter, if not the spirit, of the law. Some built docks that straddled the national boundary and would unload goods on the American side. British subjects, who were not bound by the embargo, would move the goods to the Canadian side of the dock and load it onto ships.

British merchants even arranged to have cargo intercepted by an American privateer—a privately owned vessel that was supposedly helping enforce the embargo. By law, the privateer's commander could dispose of a seized cargo however he chose. The commander would then hand the goods over to a British merchant in Canada and be paid for his trouble.

While some smugglers tried hard to disguise their actions, others felt no such compunction. Among those, the *Black Snake*'s crew was the most notorious. The *Black Snake* got its name from its tarred sides but got its reputation from its ability to evade capture.

With a sail and seven sets of oars, the forty-foot-long boat was fast. It had started life as a ferry. Now instead of passengers, the *Black Snake* hauled potash to Canada, one hundred barrels at a time, and earned its owners a tidy profit.

But the *Black Snake*'s luck ran out on August 3, 1808, when troops aboard the federal revenue cutter *Fly* got word that the boat was tied to shore three miles up the Winooski River in Burlington. The smugglers watched the *Fly* approach and warned the officers not to try to take the boat. Undaunted, the soldiers seized the *Fly*. The smugglers, led by Truman Mudgett of Highgate, fired on the troops, killing two of them, as well as a local man who happened on the scene. All but two of the *Black Snake*'s crew of ten were captured on the spot. The escapees were later caught near the border.

The Vermont Supreme Court convicted eight of the smugglers. One of the men, Cyrus Dean, was convicted of murder and earned the dubious distinction of becoming the first person executed by the state of Vermont. The hanging took place before a crowd of ten thousand in Burlington. Three other smugglers were ordered whipped and sentenced to ten years in the new state prison in Windsor, becoming the facility's first inmates.

Despite the example made of the *Black Snake*'s crew, smuggling wouldn't stop until 1814, when the United State signed a peace treaty with Britain to end the war that had erupted two years earlier. With peace, the United States lifted the embargo, and smuggling became what it had been before, merely trade.

THE YEAR WITHOUT A SUMMER

1816

PEOPLE WOULD LATER CALL 1816 "the year without a summer," "the poverty year," "the famine year," "the scarce year," and "eighteen hundred and froze to death," but it started benignly enough.

By all accounts, the winter was mild, with little snow cover after the start of the year. High temperatures in January and February reached 46 degrees, and March hit 52. An April heat wave drove the temperature to 82. Only in retrospect would people realize that the state was experiencing what one historian called "a backwards spring." Instead of warm weather blossoming as the season moved toward summer, Vermont experienced hard frosts on the nights of May 15 through 17. June started promisingly. On June 5, southern New England saw thermometers reach the 90s. Even in Vermont, temperatures rose well into the 80s.

But everything changed that night. Winds shifted from the south to the northwest, bringing a cold front from Canada. By the next morning, temperatures had plunged 40 to 50 degrees from their highs the day before.

A diarist in Brookfield, believed to be a man named Rufus C. Hovey, would record the drastic weather: "June 6, 1816: The fifth very hot, the sixth very cold, and snowed all day long. The ground and other things began to freeze at one of the clock in the day time."

The weather took hold. On June 8, the diarist wrote: "Froze all day. Ground covered with snow all day. . . . All the trees on the high land turned black." That same day, Bennington farmer Benjamin Haywood wrote: "The awful scene continued. Sweeping blasts from the North all the forepart of the day."

The *North Star* newspaper of Danville reported that on the morning of June 8 "a kind of sleet or exceeding[ly] cold snow fell, attended with high wind, which measured in places where it was drifted, 18 or 20 inches in depth . . . the weather was more severe than it generally is during the storms of winter." By June 11, the Brookfield diarist was writing, "The apple trees have wilted, and the ground is froze."

James Winchester, who was fourteen at the time, remembered the summer of 1816 as the time "when people froze to death in the month of roses—suicides through fear that the sun was cooling off." Winchester told how his uncle had ventured out into a snowstorm on June 17 to tend his sheep, saying to his wife, "If I'm not back in an hour, call the neighbors and come after me. June is a bad month to be buried in the snow, especially so near July!" Winchester reported that his uncle never returned, and wasn't found until three days later—dead, frozen, and buried in snow, a mile in the wrong direction from home.

Historians believe Winchester's story belongs in the category of folklore. Things were bad, but not *that* bad. People tended to embellish the facts in retelling the troubles of 1816. Or, like Winchester, who was in his nineties when recalling those days, perhaps simply confused them.

Perhaps most dismaying about the freakish weather was that it kept giving signs of relenting. Starting June 11, Vermont saw ten straight days of high temperatures in the 70s and 80s. Then a heat wave hit on June 22 through 24. The temperature reached 99 degrees.

The weather in July was closer to normal, except that evening temperatures were decidedly cool, which didn't help the already suffering corn crop. Hay production was also hurt. Vermont even experienced two nights of light frosts on July 8 and 9. Worse, the state saw virtually no rain between June 15 and July 17.

Things seemed to return to normal in August as seasonably warm weather prevailed during the first three weeks. Temperatures reached the 90s in some spots on July 18 and 19. Then an ill wind blew, bringing cold weather and periodic heavy frosts during the next ten days. A newspaper reported that a severe frost on August 28 "put an end to the hopes of many corn growers," who instead cut and chopped the crop for animal fodder.

September continued the cold, dry trend, which was becoming more of a rut. Heavy frosts blanketed the region during the last week of the month. Temperatures at sunrise were as low as 20 degrees that week. Relief finally arrived in October when the state was blessed with a bout of Indian summer, bringing temperatures into the mid-70s.

The wintry summer of 1816, coupled with more cold weather the next two years, infected Vermonters with what was called "Ohio fever," the only symptom of which was the strong urge to move west. Vermonters had heard about the fertile lands of the frontier, and for some of them, this weather settled it; they were moving.

Despite the ravaged crops, a famine didn't occur. While corn became expensive, meat grew cheaper as farmers, fearing they could not feed their animals, slaughtered livestock in great numbers. In the upper Connecticut River Valley, people called 1817 "the mackerel year." Businessmen, sensing an opportunity, began shipping fish inland to Vermonters wanting to supplement their diets. In some areas, fishermen found ready buyers for their catch. People from hill communities would travel to town and trade maple sugar for fish.

Some entrepreneurs took advantage of the situation. A Newbury man sold a boatload of corn for five times the normal rate. Others responded more humanely to the situation. Thomas Bellows of Bellows Falls sold seed corn to his neighbors in need. He asked only the usual price, though he certainly could have charged far more.

As to what had brought on this bizarre weather, one popular theory held that the cold winds had been caused by a large iceberg floating in the Atlantic—this despite the fact that most of the cold weather had come from the north and west.

Another contemporary explanation for the frigid weather was probably correct—a massive eruption of the volcanic Tambora, in what is today Indonesia, blew between thirty-seven and one hundred cubic *miles* of debris into the atmosphere. That was enough to drastically change weather patterns and trigger the "year without a summer."

THE *PHOENIX* STEAMBOAT DISASTER

1819

THE SMALL FLICKER OF LIGHT MIGHT HAVE SEEMED INNOCUOUS, pretty even, set against the darkness of Lake Champlain during the early morning of September 5, 1819. But the flickering soon sparked the worst maritime accident in the lake's history.

John Howard was the first to notice the light and realize it meant trouble. Howard was one of forty-five passengers and crew aboard the *Phoenix,* a steamboat headed from Burlington to Plattsburgh, New York.

Howard may have seen the glow first because he had reason to be especially alert that night. He was carrying a valuable package. The Bank of Burlington had asked him to carry $8,000—then a huge sum—to Montreal. Burlington bankers knew him as proprietor of the city's Howard Hotel and had entrusted him with this important but seemingly simple errand. Suddenly, it was becoming much more difficult.

Howard rushed to wake the other passengers, who were segregated into a gentlemen's and a ladies' cabin. Men and women poured onto deck in their nightclothes with whatever other clothing they managed to pull on in their hurry.

Among those awakened was Richard Sherman. Like Howard, Sherman had extra reason for concern. Though he was only twenty-one, Sherman was captaining the boat in place of its usual commander, his father, Jehaziel, who was home, sick in bed. Tonight, the fate of the *Phoenix* was Richard's problem.

The fire apparently started at the center of the boat, in the pantry, where, after finishing a meal, a crew member had left a candle burning untended on a shelf. The pantry sat near the boiler. Over the years, heat from the boiler had dried out the pantry's woodwork. That night, it burned like kindling. When fire reached oil that had dripped from the engine, the whole center of the boat burst into flames.

Howard stood on deck, clutching the carpetbag containing the bank's money, while his son, D. D., helped Captain Sherman try to recover money that had been stowed in the captain's office. They managed to climb over the wheelhouse, but found the office already enveloped in flames. A steady breeze from the northeast fanned the fire. The boat was doomed.

Within about five minutes, twenty people, including all the female passengers, had been lowered into the starboard lifeboat. As they were loading the boat, the stewardess, a Mrs. Wilson, hurried back to the ladies' cabin to fetch their belongings. As the lifeboat shoved off, Wilson chose to stay on board to help load the portside lifeboat, which was large enough to hold the remaining passengers and crew.

As people immediately began boarding the other lifeboat, Wilson ran downstairs to gather her own things. After only fourteen people had made it into the lifeboat, someone cut the line securing it, stranding eleven others aboard the burning steamer. Several claimed it was the engineer, a man identified today simply as MacVane.

The nearest land was Providence Island, just off South Hero, two miles away. When people aboard the lifeboat demanded that they return to rescue the others, MacVane allegedly threatened to "knock the first man overboard who should rise to make the attempt."

Those left on the *Phoenix* knew the water was their only chance. John Howard, who had sent D. D. in one of the boats with his moneybag, remained onboard with Captain Sherman. The two began throwing benches, tables, boards—anything that would float—into the water. One by one, the stranded passengers and crew jumped or were lowered into the water, then climbed aboard one of the makeshift rafts. Someone helped Mrs. Wilson onto a pair of settees.

Sherman was the last onboard. Three-quarters of the 146-foot-long boat was ablaze when he jumped into the water and climbed atop a table leaf. Sherman saw another survivor, Austin Wright, floating in the distance and shouted that he was trying to paddle to nearby Stave Island.

Meanwhile, the people in the lifeboats were rowing for Providence Island. Once they reached it and most of them had scrambled ashore, D. D. Howard led one of the lifeboats back toward the burning *Phoenix,* leaving the moneybag on the island. Colonel Harry Thomas of Burlington led the other boat back. Soon, they pulled John Howard and three other survivors into their boats. When they located Wright, he told them where Sherman was heading. They found the captain floating on his table leaf about five hundred feet from Stave Island. He had been in the water about two hours and was only partially conscious. "When I came to my senses," he said later, "I found myself in the bottom of the boat, and at once ordered my men to put about and go to the wreck in hopes of saving others."

They rowed once around the *Phoenix* and found no one. Swimming was far from a universal skill in the nineteenth century. Even many sailors couldn't swim. Nor could Mrs. Wilson. Waves knocked her into the water and she drowned. Five others also drowned that night.

The abandoned *Phoenix* drifted for miles and finally ran aground on Colchester Reef, where it burned to the waterline. People in Burlington who had seen the burning boat stockpiled supplies for the survivors at the wharves. Several boat captains loaded the goods onto their vessels and sailed in the early morning to Providence Island. Grand Isle residents also knew of the tragedy and ferried supplies to the island.

One of the passengers, described in accounts merely as "an Irishman," was particularly eager to catch a ride to Grand Isle. (Whether the man truly was Irish or the description was the result of the pervasive anti-Irish sentiment at the time is unknown.) The man had taken advantage of the chaos that night to steal the bank's money. Once on Grand Isle, he planned to catch a ferry to New York State and disappear.

Despite his harrowing experience, John Howard hadn't forgotten about the money. He dispatched another son, Sion, to fetch it. Learning that it and one of the passengers were missing, Sion set off in pursuit. He caught up with the thief near the Grand Isle ferry. The thief pulled two knives and threatened Sion, who grabbed a nearby fence stake and told the man to surrender. On this day, for some reason, one fence stake trumped two knives. The thief returned the money to Sion.

Rumors soon spread that the blaze had been no accident. The *Phoenix,* some suggested, had been sabotaged by competing shipping interests. Relations between the owners of sailing ships and the steamers were not good. Gideon King, a Burlington shipping magnate, had been known to sail one of his boats around the *Phoenix* and yell insults about how slow the boat was. In reality, the new steam-driven boats, of which the *Phoenix* was only the second on Lake

Champlain, were a looming threat to sailboats. They were larger and more dependable, since they did not rely on the wind for power.

Like the fire aboard the *Phoenix,* rumors about the cause of its demise eventually died down. Today, historians generally believe the fire was caused by nothing more sinister than a candle.

THE BOORN "MURDER" MYSTERY

1819

Stephen Boorn knew he would die soon. In fact, he knew when—January 28, 1820. That was his date with the hangman.

Everyone in Manchester knew that he and his brother, Jesse, had killed their brother-in-law, Russell Colvin. People had speculated about it for years, and now a jury had proved them right. The brothers were sentenced to death, though the Vermont Legislature had reduced Jesse's sentence to life.

As his execution date neared, Stephen swore he hadn't done it. "I am as innocent as Jesus Christ!" he told a visiting minister who had encouraged him to confess. "I don't mean that I am as guiltless as He was, I know I am a great sinner, but I am as innocent of killing Colvin as He was."

If he was so innocent, people wondered, *why had he confessed?*

The answer, like everything else in the case, is complicated.

The trouble started when the Boorns' sister, Sally, married Russell Colvin. He wasn't a great catch. By all accounts, he was a bit deranged and, even when coherent, wasn't particularly bright. Worse yet, people said he drank a lot, and that was by nineteenth-century standards.

Still, the Boorns' father, Barney, decided to help Sally and her difficult husband. They would live on the family homestead, he declared, while the brothers fended for themselves. Jealous, the Boorn boys began feuding with Colvin. Then, one day in May 1812, Colvin vanished. At first, people didn't think much about it: He'd wandered away before.

This time his disappearance stretched into months. After three years, Sally became pregnant and people knew it wasn't Colvin's child. The law prevented her from collecting support from the father if she had become pregnant while her husband was alive. Sally needed Colvin dead, at least in the eyes of the law, so she finally began a halfhearted effort to find him.

Stephen and Jesse told Sally that she could collect support from the child's father, because Colvin was indeed dead. He had gone to hell and was "where potatoes would not freeze," Stephen said cryptically. People, naturally, began to suspect foul play and assume the Boorn brothers were involved. They professed their innocence. The words about hell and potatoes had been just talk, Stephen said. They had been working with Colvin that day in 1812, he remembered, and Colvin had just walked into the woods and vanished. No, he corrected himself, they had actually been working on different farms that day. Colvin had eaten supper at home that day, Stephen went on, then he had left the house and never been seen again. As Stephen struggled with the facts, the noose seemed to tighten.

He was all but hung when his uncle Amos began telling people in town that he had been visited by Colvin's ghost, who took him to a cellar hole in a potato field. This, people decided, must have been the place where "potatoes would not freeze" and they excavated it at once. Inside, they found pieces of crockery, a button, a penknife, and a jackknife, but no human remains. Sally identified the items as her husband's.

A few days later, a fire broke out in the Boorns' sheep barn. This must be related to the murder, people figured. Then a dog unearthed some charred bones in an old tree stump. Three local physicians compared the bones to a recently amputated leg and declared them human. Amateur detectives in town had the case cracked. The Boorn boys had killed Colvin and buried him in the cellar hole. Sometime later, they had decided they should move the body to the barn, where they had tried to burn it. They had then hidden the remaining pieces in the stump. The authorities had all the evidence they needed. Jesse was arrested and constables searched for Stephen, who had recently moved to New York State.

Jesse's cell-mate, a forger named Silas Merrill, told authorities that Jesse had confessed. According to Merrill, Jesse admitted that Stephen had bludgeoned Colvin with a club during an argument. While Colvin was lying on the ground, Barney Boorn had happened by and decided to finish Colvin off with Stephen's penknife. Then, Merrill said, the Boorns had disposed of the body just as townspeople had conjectured. For this information, Merrill won his release.

Feeling the noose around his own neck, Jesse confessed, but gave himself a smaller role in the deed, perhaps hoping to save his life. Apparently thinking his brother was out of harm's way in New York, Jesse exonerated his father and pinned most of the blame on Stephen. At about this time, Stephen was headed back to Vermont. A Manchester constable had tracked him down and he had agreed to return to clear his name. Learning that Stephen had been caught, Jesse recanted.

The trial went badly for the Boorns. Witness after witness testified about the hostility between the brothers and Colvin, about threats the brothers had made, and about how the three had been working together on the day in question. Under the strain, Stephen confessed. But he said Colvin had hit him first, perhaps believing that the mitigating circumstance of self-defense would save his neck.

It didn't work. The jury was not deterred, even after the physicians declared that upon further review the bones, the key evidence, were definitely *not* human. So Stephen Boorn sat in his cell, praying for a miracle.

As Stephen's execution loomed, James Whelpley, a Manchester native then living in New York City, met a man working at a nearby farm. The man had arrived in town using the name Russell Colvin, but had since changed it. Whelpley struck up a conversation and quickly realized the farmhand knew Manchester intimately. This, Whelpley realized, must be the missing man he'd read about in the newspapers.

But Colvin refused to return to Manchester. Whelpley, however, was able to coax Colvin into a stagecoach, as part of a ruse in which Whelpley was going to introduce Colvin to a young woman. Instead, Whelpley essentially kidnapped Colvin and took him back to Manchester.

They arrived on December 22, a month ahead of Stephen's execution date. Word of their arrival had preceded them and a crowd gathered at Black's Tavern, where the stage stopped, to see if it really was Colvin. Stephen Boorn was brought before Colvin in leg irons. Colvin seemed surprised to see his brother-in-law and asked why he was in chains. In the most memorable sentence of his life, the now-vindicated Stephen said, "Because they say I murdered you."

THE MILLERITE MISCALCULATION

1844

As MIDNIGHT APPROACHED ON MARCH 21, 1844, a farmer in Rutland climbed on his barn roof, then, sporting a pair of homemade wings, awaited the hour of reckoning. When it came, the farmer took a literal leap of faith off the barn and, he prayed, into the arms of his Lord. The strangest thing about the farmer—whose name has been lost to history, but whose deed was recalled by his neighbor—is that his behavior did not stand out from the strange way countless others were acting in 1843 and 1844.

Vermont, like areas around the country, was in the thrall of William Miller and his prediction that the Second Coming of Christ was imminent. Miller's following was so strong that even those who mocked him could be excused for glancing nervously skyward on the appointed day.

Miller's prediction created a national phenomenon, but it had roots closer to home. Growing up in Poultney, he was said by some to have been an atheist. Others claimed he was a deist, and thereby believed that God created the world but wasn't involved in how it functions. Deist or atheist, he wasn't the sort you'd think would lead a religious movement.

Miller made a sudden conversion during the War of 1812. Some link the change to the suffering he saw on the battlefield, which made him think of the hereafter. Others chalk up his new thinking to a serious head wound he suffered during the war. Whatever the cause, Miller began reading the Bible methodically, searching for revelations. After years of contemplation, he came up with a stunner. According to his reading, Judgment Day was coming, and he believed he knew when. By following clues he said were in the Bible, Miller announced that it would occur sometime "around 1843."

Ordinarily the prophecies of a solitary, self-styled biblical scholar would have gone nowhere. But at the time, social conditions in the United States were ripe for that kind of message. The nation was still feeling the effects of the Second Great Awakening, the religious movement that swept through the Northeast beginning in the 1820s. Preachers were urgently declaring that the Millennium—Christ's return to Earth—was at hand.

In 1831, Miller, who had been without a pulpit, got the call to fill in for an ill pastor. Miller revealed his prediction to his congregation but said several things had to occur first: The Earth would tremble, wars would break out, mankind's genius would make significant progress, and people would see marvels in the sky.

Quickly his predictions seemed to be coming true: As they predictably do, earthquakes and wars continued to happen. Furthermore, the United States was in the midst of creating unprecedented technological wonders, such as the Erie Canal.

When, on the night of November 13, 1833, a massive meteor shower hit the Earth, Miller began to look pretty smart. Preachers, perhaps as many as a thousand of them, began to spread his prophecy and win converts. Eventually, an estimated one hundred thousand people joined Miller's cause.

As 1843 approached, people reacted with a mixture of hope and dread. Miller had never set a date for Judgment Day, but followers said it would come at the start of spring, March 21. In Vermont, believers stopped making plans beyond that date. They gave away their property. They abandoned their fields. Why not? The Lord was coming and they would never need food or possessions again.

On the appointed day, Millerites everywhere gathered. In Wardsboro, a group assembled in the graveyard, crying and yelling in excitement. With them was the shrouded body of a woman who had recently died. Like others in the region, her family believed that burying the dead would only delay their rendezvous with God. In Calais, Millerites, after giving away their possessions, climbed up on the roof of their church. There, dressed in white "ascension robes," they prayed and waited.

When the sun rose the next morning on an unchanged world, they descended to the hoots of amused onlookers. It was hard to say which was worse—the derision, the disillusionment, or the sudden poverty.

The anticipated "Great Reckoning" had become "the Great Disappointment."

Eventually, the phrase would encompass two more dates. Miller responded to criticism by saying that the date had been right but the year wrong. Judgment Day would come on March 21, 1844.

Similar disappointment greeted dawn on the morning of March 22, 1844. At which point, Miller rechecked his figures and declared that the true day would be October 22, 1844. That date, of course, proved no more prophetic.

Perhaps Miller understood that his predictions had a wide margin of error. As the supposed Judgment Days came and went, he is said to have built new stone walls on his property and kept his larder well stocked.

Around Vermont and the rest of the Northeast, followers eventually lost faith in Miller. As nineteen-year-old Harriet Hutchinson of East Braintree explained in a letter to her fiancé dated December 1, 1844: "Miller's project has failed, Millerism is pretty much down about here. I think it has done a great deal of injury—there were some that did not harvest their grain until very late if they have at all, they were so sure the world would come to an end this fall . . . and they should not want any more provision, therefore their families are made destitute."

Hutchinson refused to mock the Millerites. "I had my fears about it [that Miller was right]," she confessed, "but never was a believer, very far from it."

After Miller's third failure, few of his believers remained. Yet many retained their faith in more traditional religion. Among them was that farmer from Rutland. His fall broke his leg, but not his spirit. He gave up on Miller but remained devout enough to become a deacon in his local church.

THE PHINEAS GAGE ACCIDENT

1848

PHINEAS GAGE WILL ALWAYS BE REMEMBERED for what happened to him on September 13, 1848. By all rights, he should have died. In a way, part of him did.

That day, he was directing blasting in Cavendish for the Rutland & Burlington Railroad, which was laying tracks through the town. It was tricky and dangerous work, but after hours and days of repetition, people can lose their focus. That's what happened to Gage.

His job involved creating an explosive charge by pouring powder into a drilled hole, dropping in a fuse, and gently tamping it with a heavy metal rod, before pouring in sand and then tamping more vigorously to form a plug that would direct the force of the eventual explosion down into the rock.

Writing later with extreme understatement, one Gage researcher observed that: "Where the material being drilled is of a kind that the impact of an iron bar upon it is likely to generate a spark and the explosive charge is susceptible to being so ignited, the use of a crowbar is somewhat imprudent"—as Gage was to learn.

The tamping iron in Gage's hand was three-and-a-half feet long, more than an inch in diameter, and weighed more than thirteen pounds. The accident occurred when he either dropped the bar or, believing the sand had already been added, plunged it too hard into the hole. The resulting explosion shot the heavy rod upward like a bullet.

An instant before the explosion, Gage had turned his head to watch his men working in a pit behind him. That turn saved his life, but shattered it too.

The rod shot through his left cheek, passed behind his left eye and out through the top of his head, landing nearly one hundred feet away. The impact knocked Gage to the ground, where he lay convulsing for a few moments. His men rushed to him and assumed he was in his death throes, but minutes later he began to speak to them.

Stunned that he was still alive, the men decided to carry him by oxcart to the local tavern to see if anything could be done. Gage insisted on walking to the cart. And when it reached town, he climbed down and walked to the tavern's veranda to await the doctor who had been summoned.

The first doctor to arrive, a Dr. Williams from Proctorsville, examined the wound at the top of Gage's head, which he said resembled "an inverted funnel." He didn't believe Gage's story that a rod had shot through his head until Gage pointed to the small slit in his cheek. Supporting Gage's version of events was the rod itself, which was found about twenty-five yards from the spot of the explosion, smeared with blood and brains.

Next to arrive was Dr. John Harlow, who took over Gage's care. He cleaned the wound, picking out the smaller bone shards and leaving the larger ones to stitch themselves back together. When in the coming days Gage refused to take Harlow's orders to remain in bed, the doctor laid him low with doses of "calomel, rhubarb and caster oil."

Harlow attributed Gage's recovery to God and the body's own resilience (which he called by the Latin term "vis conservatrix"). Twenty years later, in a booklet titled bluntly *Recovery from the Passage of an Iron Bar through the Head,* Harlow wrote:

> *For what surgeon, the most skilful, with all the blandishments of his art, has the world ever known, who could presume to take one of his fellows who has had so formidable a missile hurled through his brain, with a crash and bring him, without the aid of this vis conservatrix, so that, on the fifty-sixth day thereafter, he would have been walking in the streets again?*

News of the accident reached the general public about a week after it occurred. Two Boston newspapers reported the incident under the headline "Horrible Accident." Two days later, the *Vermont Mercury* of Woodstock ran the headline "Wonderful Accident," focusing on the wonder that Gage had survived so long, though the paper assumed Gage had little chance of living much longer.

An A. Angier of Cavendish wrote the *Boston Christian Reflector* and *Christian Watchman* about the astonishing incident:

> *We live in an eventful era, but if a man can have thirteen pounds of iron in the shape of a pointed bar, thrown through his head, carrying with it a quantity of the brain, and yet live and have his senses, we may well exclaim, What next?*

The excitement over Gage's recovery, however, was overblown. In many ways, he died the instant the tamping iron struck his brain. Before the accident, Gage had been known for his level-headedness and hard work. Afterward, Harlow wrote, Gage "was no longer Gage." Even casual acquaintances noticed the change. Gage tried to return to work with the railroad but proved unreliable and was let go. He became combative and irresponsible. People reported seeing him walking around in shirtsleeves on cold, rainy days.

Gage's erratic behavior has led researchers to realize that different areas of the brain control different functions. The frontal lobes, to which Gage suffered grievous injury, regulate personality. But scientists were slow to come to that conclusion. At the time, it was unthinkable that something as abhorrent as immoral behavior could have be linked to a physical cause.

Gage worked for a time in a stable, then began to wander through New England's larger cities and towns and eventually found his way to New York, where he became a living part of P. T. Barnum's museum. He drifted to Chile, where he tended horses for a stagecoach company. Later, he moved to San Francisco and worked on area farms. He began having seizures and eventually died from one in May 1861—twelve-and-a-half years after his accident.

Today, Gage's skull is part of the teaching collection at Harvard University's Warren Anatomical Museum. Displayed with it is the crowbar that Gage had kept as a souvenir of the day he cheated death in Cavendish.

A COUNTERFEITING SCHEME

1850

A CONVERSATION CHANGED CHRISTIAN MEADOWS'S LIFE FOREVER. Apparently a decent fellow—hardworking, respectful, and generally honest—Meadows found himself buttonholed by the aptly named Ephraim Low, a failed storekeeper from the town of Groton. Low was hatching a plot and needed a man of Meadows's talents to pull it off. Whatever he said, Low was persuasive.

Arriving in Groton one day in 1850, Meadows made his way to a small farmhouse Low owned outside the village, where he would board. Meadows had until recently worked as an engraver for a Boston print shop. Dies used for printing bank notes had recently disappeared and soon thereafter so had Meadows. It was no coincidence. Low had convinced Meadows to make the leap from honest engraver to counterfeiter. He soon became the most famous counterfeiter in the region, which was not necessarily a good thing.

When Meadows took up counterfeiting, he was following a long, if not proud, tradition in Vermont. The state had always been awash in counterfeit bills, the practice having started even before Vermont's founding in 1777. The federal government didn't have a monopoly on printing money in those days. State and private banks printed their own. The abundance of currencies made life easy for counterfeiters. With so many types of bills circulating through the economy, the average citizen was hard-pressed to spot a fake. That's what Meadows, Low, and their fellow collaborators were banking on.

Meadows was part of an odd assortment of characters that descended on the rural town over the course of several days during 1850. As writer Stephen Greene explained in his book *Mischief in the Mountains,* Meadows was one of three men with British accents who suddenly appeared in town.

Meadows was joined by his wife, who arrived with their baby. Another Brit greeted the arrival of his "wife," a woman who dressed in a showy, urban style, quite different from the farmwife's life she was supposedly adopting in Groton.

The gang picked Groton because it was a backwater, far from nosy authorities. How they thought they would go unnoticed in a small town is less obvious. The plan, as devised by Low, called for Meadows to take authentic bank notes, erase the denominations, and print higher numbers in their places. The two other British men—William Warburton, known as Bristol Bill for a bank heist he once committed, and George Green, a burglar and one-time boxer—were to pass the completed notes.

Low's job, in addition to recruiting gang members, was to gather the printing equipment they would need. But Meadows soon learned that Low was no better a counterfeiter than he had been a storeowner. The press lacked crucial parts.

While the others waited, Low hustled to Boston to obtain the missing pieces. Warburton grew impatient, so he used his time to try a few burglaries. When he learned that state bank commissioners were visiting St. Johnsbury to collect deposits for the new Passumpsic

Bank, Warburton took his supposed wife, former cabaret singer Margaret O'Connor, with him. The couple entered the Hull Curtis Hotel, where the commissioners were staying. O'Connor immediately took over the parlor piano and launched into song. While she entertained the bank officials, Warburton slipped upstairs and rifled through their things, but came away empty-handed.

Warburton met similar failure when he attempted to rob banks in Montpelier, Danville, Chelsea, Irasburg, and across the border in Stanstead, Quebec. All were better guarded than he had expected.

Vermont proved less hospitable than the gang members had hoped. On a tip from Meadows's former employer, who had somehow tracked him to Goshen, police arrested Warburton, O'Connor, Meadows and his wife, as well as Low and two other local men. They also seized the burglars' tools, a pair of presses, a store of dies, and one bank note that had had its denomination chemically removed.

After their arrests, gang members met different fates. Officials dismissed charges against the two women. Two local accomplices testified for the state and were treated leniently. Low died of pleurisy, a lung ailment, before his trial.

Meadows and Warburton were tried together and convicted. When the judge ordered them both to serve ten years hard labor at the state prison in Windsor, Meadows sat in shock, comforted by his wife. As the state's attorney, Bliss Davis, leaned over to speak with Meadows, an outraged Warburton drew a hidden knife and stabbed Davis in the neck. Davis, miraculously, survived, the knife having missed his jugular.

Meadows and Warburton were taken off to prison to begin serving their sentences. Warburton would have to return to face trial for his brutal attack.

Once at Windsor, Meadows sought to regain his respectability. Prison officials let him resume work as an engraver, and word of his prowess soon spread in the surrounding community. Dartmouth College and the New Hampshire State Agricultural Society hired him to do work for them while he did time. Secretary of State Daniel Webster, of New Hampshire, loved the seal Meadows had created for the society so much that he wrote Vermont's governor, suggesting the talented man be pardoned.

In 1853, Governor Erastus Fairbanks took up the suggestion and pardoned Meadows. He even gave Meadows and his wife $100 toward buying a house in Vermont. Meadows returned to his life as an honest engraver, having become convinced that there were better ways to make money than making money.

A BREAKTHROUGH FOR WOMEN

1852

CLARINA HOWARD NICHOLS'S VOICE CRACKED IN NERVOUSNESS. Her heart pounded. She felt faint, and she briefly rested her head on her hand. But she kept speaking, and her words—indeed her very presence—changed Vermont.

The year was 1852, and Nichols was standing behind the speaker's podium in the Vermont House. Though the state had been founded sixty-one years earlier, she was the first woman to address the Legislature.

Nichols faced an unfriendly crowd that evening as she spoke for women's rights. The lawmakers, all of whom were male, of course, had begrudgingly invited her after she'd collected more than two hundred signatures from prominent Brattleboro businessmen and others, asking that she be given a hearing. The only other women there were packed into the gallery, and Nichols wasn't sure they were on her side, women's rights being such a new concept.

Still, Nichols mustered the courage to stand before the lawmakers and argue for a sliver of equality for women—specifically, that they be allowed to vote at school meetings. The chairman of the House Education Committee, Joseph H. Barrett, had dared Nichols to come. "If the lady wants to make herself ridiculous, let her come and make herself as ridiculous as possible and as soon as possible," he declared, "but I don't believe in this scramble for the breeches!"

Opponents of women's rights often claimed that women like Nichols wanted to take on the attributes of men, right down to their clothing. Barrett had even threatened to humiliate Nichols after her speech by presenting her with a suit of men's clothes. Barrett's "breeches" comment was well known by the time Nichols spoke, and she used it deftly to remind lawmakers just how few rights women had, especially involving property. In her closing remarks, Nichols recalled years later, she had said "[though I] had earned the dress I wore, my husband owned it—not of his own will, but by a law adopted by bachelors and other women's husbands."

How could lawmakers claim that women wanted to wear men's pants, she asked, when it was the lawmakers themselves "who have legislated our skirts into *their* possession." By law, single women had the same property rights as men. But, once married, a woman ceded her property to her husband. He could sell her clothes, take any money she earned, and send any children she had from a previous marriage to the poorhouse. And she had no right to vote to change the laws that oppressed her.

Though Nichols couldn't vote, she knew her words could have an impact. In fact, in 1847, her writings had convinced lawmakers to protect married women's real estate from their husbands' debts and to allow them to write wills.

Nichols brought a passion to her work that may have grown out of her religious faith and bad first marriage. Born into a prominent family in West Townshend, Nichols showed early on that she was a person of strong beliefs. At the age of eight, she proclaimed her faith and joined the Baptist church. When she was twenty, she married a man named Justin Carpenter and moved with him to western New York, where she taught at a seminary for young women. Nine years and three children later, she moved back to Vermont and filed for divorce. In an era when divorce was considered scandalous, it was a desperate move. She claimed she had suffered "intolerable severity," or abuse. Carpenter had apparently done little to support his family. Indeed, for years Nichols had sustained her husband and children with money she earned from teaching and writing. Few doubted that Carpenter was at fault. His parents even backed Nichols in the divorce.

As a single mother, Nichols supported her family by writing for the *Windham County Democrat* in Brattleboro. Four years later, she married the paper's editor, George Nichols, who was twenty-eight years her senior. Still, it proved a good match.

George Nichols apparently encouraged his wife's independent streak and relied on her to help produce the paper. Soon after they married, he grew sick and she gradually took over as editor, though she wouldn't publicly acknowledge her position for years. When she finally revealed that she was the editor, Nichols started getting invited to speak at women's rights conventions in the Northeast and as far west as Wisconsin. Her words seem revolutionary, coming as they did more than a century before the days of the women's rights movement.

Nichols told a crowd in Worcester, Massachusetts, in 1851 that ever since she was a child, "I could not believe that God had created so many homely women," she said, "and suffered all to lose their beauty in the very maturity of their powers, and yet made it our duty to spend our best efforts trying to look pretty." In other words, women weren't put on Earth to look beautiful. Rather than worry about looks, she encouraged them to "cultivate . . . your powers of mind and heart."

The next year brought Nichols her chance to speak to the Legislature and brought Vermont its chance to show itself ahead of the times. But lawmakers squandered the opportunity, refusing to allow women the vote on school issues. Women wouldn't get the right to vote in school elections until 1880, at town meetings until 1917, and in statewide elections until 1920.

Nichols's speech didn't change any laws, but it started to change some minds—perhaps none more so than those of the women in the Statehouse gallery. These were middle-class women who were well supported by their husbands and risked losing their status by changing the system. But they were won over by Nichols's speech. They rushed to greet her beside the speaker's desk and one of them said, "We didn't know before what women's rights were, Mrs. Nichols, but we are for women's rights."

THE ST. ALBANS RAID

1864

PEOPLE'S FIRST THOUGHT MIGHT HAVE BEEN that the young man was joking, or else that he was insane. He stood on the steps of the American House hotel in St. Albans, a revolver in his hand, shouting, "This city is now in the possession of the Confederate States of America."

He was, however, deadly serious. Lieutenant Bennett Young and about twenty of his fellow Confederates had slipped into town in the fall of 1864 to rob banks, burn buildings, terrify the citizenry, and kill them if need be. A rebel attack was the last thing on people's minds that day. By that point in the Civil War, the military campaign had moved south of the Mason-Dixon Line.

For the roughly thirty minutes it took the Confederates to rob three banks, St. Albans was in turmoil. Many residents, apparently having missed Young's brief pronouncement, weren't even sure who was attacking the city or why. The *St. Albans Messenger*'s edition that day—October 19, 1864—reported that the city had been "invaded" and its banks robbed by a "party of about twenty-five." The paper, in its haste to get the news out or in all the confusion, neglected to mention that the raiders had been Confederates.

Young later claimed that he and others in his party had removed their overcoats to reveal Confederate uniforms beneath. If they did, few seemed to notice. What they might have noticed was small groups of young men entering the banks on Main Street or others who seemed to be rounding up horses.

The Confederates had planned the assault in Quebec and had drifted over the border in twos and threes during the last few days to avoid suspicion. They had picked St. Albans after learning that a horse buyer for the Union Army would be in town to purchase a number of Morgans, the breed for which Vermont was famous and which had served the Army well. The raiders knew the banks would be especially well stocked after the purchase.

With his revolver drawn, Young and several raiders entered the First National Bank while groups of four headed toward the nearby Franklin County Bank and the St. Albans Bank. Just as Young entered First National, a man walked out. Seeing the gun, he shouted, "They're robbing the bank!" A Confederate grabbed the man and another yelled that he should be shot. But Young ordered one of his soldiers to take the man across the street to the village green, where a growing number of citizens would soon be held under armed guard.

Young and his men stole much of the gold and currency they found in the bank. As they were preparing to leave, a local merchant who was the town's gold buyer arrived at the bank. The Confederates quickly stashed their pistols, and Young coolly asked the man, James Russell Armington, whether he wished to buy any gold. Not realizing he had walked into the midst of a robbery, Armington struck a deal with Young, who apparently wanted something lighter than gold when he made his escape.

Down the street, a group led by Confederate lieutenant William Hutchinson entered the Franklin County Bank with guns concealed. Hutchinson asked the clerk whether the bank had gold to sell. Told they would have to see Armington, Hutchinson replied, "Well, the hell with Mr. Armington" and pointed his pistol at the clerk.

Then he ordered the clerk and the bank's president, who had been in a back office, to swear allegiance to the Confederacy and its president, Jefferson Davis. When the clerk balked, Hutchinson cocked his revolver. The two bank officials took the pledge. Hutchinson and company left with all the cash, securities, and gold they could stuff into their large carpetbags. At the third bank, raiders locked the clerk in the airtight safe. Minutes later, however, passersby arrived at the bank to see what the commotion was and managed to open the safe.

As the minutes passed, the Confederates became more nervous and the people of St. Albans less so. Soon, people began taking shots at the raiders. One man grabbed his revolver and stalked the Confederates, firing at them three times—only to have his gun misfire each time. Another man shot at Young from an upstairs window but missed. Young did not. The man slumped across the windowsill, badly injured. Two others were shot during the raid. One suffered only a flesh wound, but the other later died of his wounds.

Then the Confederates tried to burn down the town. Grabbing forty bottles of explosive chemicals prepared for this moment, they rode along Main Street, hurling them at buildings. As the bottles burst into flame, the raiders whooped. But many of the firebombs failed to explode and the explosives did little more than burn down a shed.

Word spread that the raiders were going to attack the home of Governor J. Gregory Smith. The governor was at work in Montpelier, but his wife grabbed a large revolver and stood guard, awaiting an assault that never came.

The Confederates had instead decided to flee to Canada. Minutes later, a posse took up the chase and gained quickly. When the raiders reached Sheldon, they burned a bridge but had no time to rob the town's bank as planned. Likewise, they scrapped a raid on Swanton.

The Confederates crossed into Canada. The posse followed, soon managing to capture several raiders, including Young. Canadian authorities caught others and demanded that all the captive raiders be left in Canada. A Canadian court eventually ordered the men released, ruling that their actions were legal during wartime.

The raiders had wanted to get money for the cash-strapped Confederacy. They stole about $200,000, but lost most or all of it in their hasty retreat and eventual capture. Their other purpose had been to distract the Union army and slow its progress south. But the raid on the northern frontier did nothing to change the course of the war.

THE FENIAN INVASION

1866

SOMETHING WAS AFOOT IN ST. ALBANS. The 5:40 a.m. train had screeched to a halt at the depot and disgorged three hundred men. Their luggage consisted of eight wooden boxes, the *St. Albans Messenger* reported, "hardly suggestive of wearing apparel." Their business was supposed to be secret, but everyone could guess what they were up to. That winter and spring of 1866, newspapers had reported rumors of a planned attack on British-held Canada by Irish-American radicals. The Fenians, as they called themselves, had the fanciful vision of seizing Canada and using it as a base to attack British forces in Ireland and set that island free.

For several days, strangers had streamed into St. Albans. By the morning of June 1, the streets were full of men bearing Irish names. The new arrivals reminded some residents of a much smaller, and more discrete, group of strangers who had drifted into town two years earlier. Those men had turned out to be Confederates, who in the waning days of the Civil War had robbed local banks and killed a man before fleeing into Canada, from which they had come.

Now marauders were attacking in the other direction, and some Vermonters were unsympathetic to Canada's plight. After all, the Canadian government had let the Confederates "go unwhipt of justice," the *Vermont Journal* had told readers in March 1866. "It does certainly come hard to have one's ox gored," the Windsor paper wrote, but "[s]o long as it is a neighbor's, it does not seem so bad."

The Fenians, named after an ancient Irish militia, relied on Vermonters for support. Peter Ward, superintendent of St. Albans's gas works, had been busily stowing weapons. The Fenians had bought surplus army swords and rifles from the U.S. government and shipped them to Ward packed in crates marked "glass" and "gas fixtures." More arms caches were hidden in surrounding towns in the barns of supportive farmers.

As suddenly as those three hundred Fenians had arrived in St. Albans, they melted away. They were seen marching off in groups in every direction. But the next morning's train brought another crush of men from Boston and points south. In all, more than one thousand men would assemble in Franklin County during late May and early June 1866 for an attack north.

They saw themselves as the advance guard of a giant movement. The Fenian Brotherhood claimed a quarter-million adherents, and solicited donations from the country's 1.6 million Irish-Americans. In Vermont alone, about one thousand men belonged to chapters located in Burlington, Rutland, West Rutland, Bennington, Brattleboro, Windsor, Montpelier, Wells River, St. Johnsbury, Moretown, Waterbury, Northfield, and St. Albans. Six of those communities also boasted Fenian Sisterhoods, a sort of women's auxiliary.

Attacking Canada might seem quixotic at best. But the Fenians had reasons to dream. They hoped to raise an army of thousands that could quickly overwhelm the lightly guarded provinces of

Canada. And many Fenians were battle-hardened by their service in the Civil War.

They planned to attack at key spots along a thousand-mile-long front that extended as far west as Wisconsin. The troops in Vermont would form the right wing, under the direction of General Samuel Spear.

When Spear slipped into St. Albans that spring, he found that plans had gone badly awry. The volunteers were arriving without firearms. Worse, many of the guns already smuggled in lacked any ammunition that fit them.

On June 4, when Fenian secretary of war Thomas Sweeny, a one-armed Civil War hero, arrived to survey the situation, he learned that U.S. agents were intercepting firearms headed to the border. He was enraged. The government officials who had sold the Fenians the surplus weapons must have known what they'd be used for, he argued. Two days later, on June 6, things got worse for the Fenians. President Andrew Johnson warned Americans not to attack British possessions. He was spurred by Canadian outrage over a recent, though unsuccessful, raid by Fenians into Ontario. Then that night, U.S. general George Meade, who was in St. Albans to prevent just this kind of assault, went after Fenian leaders. Meade, leader of the Union victory at Gettysburg three years earlier, had Sweeny arrested at midnight in his hotel bed. Spear, who allegedly hid in the bathroom, escaped and fled to Franklin, where his men were camped.

Spear must have known his attack was now the worst-kept secret in the North Country. Fenian leaders had expected to mass eight thousand men at the Vermont border, but only about one thousand had arrived so far. Seeking to avoid American intervention, Spear ordered an immediate invasion anyway. The Fenians met little opposition at first, only a small group of Canadian militia, who wisely withdrew. The only person the militia killed was an unfortunate

Canadian woman they had mistaken for a Fenian. Soon the Fenians had marched six miles into Canada, seizing three villages along the way and planting a green flag on a hilltop.

Spear expected reinforcements and arms to flow quickly north. None came. But something was moving south. A contingent of British Army regulars, including cavalry and artillery and joined by Canadian volunteers, swept down on the Fenians. One British cavalry soldier remembered watching as an artillery unit unlimbered its guns and prepared to fire. The Fenians were watching, too. "[T]he sight," the soldier recalled, "added a poignancy to the yearning for home which was at that moment afflicting the Fenian breast."

A cavalry captain mercifully ordered his men to use only the flat sides of their swords, so the horsemen swatted at the fleeing Fenians, who got off an occasional wild shot. "In this running fight, we soon reached the boundary line," the soldier said. "There a company of United States regulars was stationed, and as fast as a Fenian tumbled over the line he was seized and disarmed."

Meade's men marched the Fenians to St. Albans, where over the following days they were put on trains headed south. By June 16, the last Fenian was gone.

Amazingly enough, the Fenians would return to northern Vermont four years later. The invasion plan was almost identical and, unfortunately for the Fenians, so too was the result.

THE BURLINGTON WINTER CARNIVAL

1886

MONTREAL'S HARDSHIP WAS BURLINGTON'S BOON. When smallpox hit the Canadian city in 1886, it inadvertently helped Vermont make a name for itself in the world of winter sports.

For the previous couple years, Montreal had hosted a hugely popular winter carnival, but the epidemic, which would kill 3,164 people, forced organizers to cancel the event. To Vermont's great good fortune, an outdoors sport group, the Burlington Coasting Club, had been planning a similar event. Outdoor sports enthusiasts, disappointed by the cancellation of Montreal's carnival, turned their eyes to Burlington.

Just the year before, the idea of Burlington hosting such an event seemed unthinkable. Mayor Urban Woodbury had banned coasting, what we would call sledding or sliding, on the city's streets. And in February 1885, the state's attorney for Chittenden County declared he would prosecute anyone caught violating the ban. He failed to follow through on that threat just days later, however, when a local man admitted to the mayor that he had been coasting. This was no ordinary resident, however. This was Dr. William Seward Webb, owner of a great estate in Shelburne, son-in-law of the Vanderbilts, and the cream of Chittenden County society.

What motivated Webb to admit his complicity in this controversial sport? Perhaps, as a leading citizen, he was embarrassed that his behavior might set a bad example. Or perhaps he thought the anti-coasting rules were silly. Perhaps he wanted the public to know that coasting was a sport, if not of kings, then of Webbs and their friends, which was as near as Vermont came to royalty.

Webb followed up his apology not by abandoning the sport but by helping formalize it. He helped found the coasting club, and became its president. A University of Vermont professor, a prominent lawyer and state senator, a bank president, and a leading manufacturer filled the club's other offices. Members of the business and professional classes—lawyers, storeowners, and the like—made up the club's membership.

The coasting club set to work, lining Main Street with torches to light the route at night, and arranging for people to monitor the course and warn passersby of oncoming sleds. The club also built a toboggan slide at the junction of St. Paul and Howard Streets and purchased toboggans for free use by members, or rental by the general public.

To foster a club identity, organizers required that, while sledding, members wear the club's uniform, which consisted of a red sash, woolen tuque, and a badge that depicted a toboggan with the club's initials overlaid.

The next fall, club members began planning their winter carnival. In addition to the predictable events of coasting and tobogganing, organizers also scheduled ice hockey games, skating races, and "a fancy skating tournament" at a newly created rink; iceboating, sleighing, and trotting races on the lake; fireworks; snowshoe races; and a club dinner and grand carnival ball.

Conditions were perfect for a successful carnival. A warm spell, which had threatened the event, ended with colder weather and light snow. Winter sports enthusiasts from along the East Coast and Canada crowded into Burlington for the festivities.

"Burlington tonight is all one vast blaze of electric lights, Chinese lanterns, and houses illuminated as though they were on fire," reported one New York City paper. "The air resounds with revelry and fun, the streets are literally jammed with people, and the sport is wilder than anything ever seen in Montreal, Orange, or even Albany."

The thrilling coast down Main Street was a major attraction, with a reported one thousand riders an hour zooming down the course. Others flocked to the lakeshore to watch the iceboat and horse races, or to skate on the rink, which was lit at night by torches.

Burlington reveled in all the attention. The event seemed to signal the city's entrance into the big time, as luminaries from around the East Coast and Quebec turned up. "[A] more brilliant assembly was never seen in Burlington, hundreds of well-known society people from other cities joining in the promenades and dances and the beauty and chivalry of our own city being fully represented," gushed the *Burlington Free Press.*

The *Boston Transcript* reported that "the magnitude of its success surpasses even the Club's wildest dreams. Burlington was made on purpose for a winter carnival."

The festivities gave every indication of becoming a major annual event. The next year's carnival also ran smoothly, despite uncooperative weather. A thaw again hit just before the opening, but this time didn't lift. And though a decent crowd turned out, the event lacked the luster of its first year. The Boston, New York, and Montreal socialites who made the first year so grand were mostly missing. Montreal's smallpox outbreak had ended and the city again hosted a winter carnival, which attracted much of the glitterati.

The Burlington Coasting Club couldn't muster the enthusiasm to host another carnival. The events put heavy demands on club members' time; and if the event wasn't going to match the glow of the first year, they had better things to do. Membership dropped precipitously. Even Webb, who had been so instrumental in starting the club, seems to have lost interest, having done little to help organize the 1887 event.

Coasting and tobogganing proved something of a fad, too. Within a few years, the Burlington Coasting Club became defunct. But if it failed to establish a Burlington winter carnival as a major annual social event, it had at least shown that Vermont could draw visitors in winter—even if it would take another half century, and the creation of ski areas, to fulfill that promise.

THE WEST HARTFORD TRAIN WRECK

1887

WHEN THE FIRST SIGNS OF TROUBLE CAME, passengers had no time to react. Shortly after leaving White River Junction, the Montreal Express suddenly began to sway and shake violently. The train was moments away from the most deadly wreck in Vermont history.

All had seemed normal just moments before. Many of the train's passengers were sleeping—it was shortly after 2:00 a.m. on February 5, 1887. Those who were awake were in fine spirits. The cars were crowded with people making the ride north through a frigid night to Canada to catch Montreal's celebrated winter carnival.

Conductor Smith Sturtevant, who had met the train at White River Junction, walked the aisles collecting tickets, laughing and joking with a friend he spotted among the passengers. No one seemed to mind that the train was an hour and a half behind schedule.

The shaking began about ten minutes north of White River, just as the train approached a bridge near West Hartford. Sturtevant knew they were in trouble. He pulled the bell cord to signal the brakeman to stop the train.

Hearing the bell, brakeman George Parker glanced toward the rear of the train. To his horror, he saw that the train was jumping the tracks. Seeing no way to stop the cars from derailing, Parker leaped from the train into deep snow. Landing on the slope of a hill, he tumbled down the embankment to the frozen White River below.

The engineer, whose name is recorded simply as Pierce, also witnessed the derailment. Looking back from his spot at the head of the train, he saw the rear sleeping car plummet off the bridge toward the river forty feet below. Still attached to the cars ahead of it, the sleeper peeled three other cars off the tracks with it. The weight of those four falling cars broke the connection with the lead cars, sparing the locomotive and the mail car.

Landing upside down on the thick ice, but not breaking through, the passenger cars shattered under the weight of their wheels. Many passengers were killed instantly in the crash. Others were trapped in the debris.

Once the train came to rest on the ice, things only got worse.

The cars were lighted by oil lamps and heated by coal stoves. After the crash, fire from the lamps and stoves ignited the wooden cars, their draperies, and upholstery. As fires erupted, Pierce, the engineer, found the brakeman, Parker, on the ice. He had survived his jump. Pierce told him to get help.

Parker made his way to a nearby farm. Borrowing a team of horses, he rode off toward White River, which was about four miles away. It would be forty-five minutes before rescuers would arrive.

In the meantime, passengers and crew members were on their own. The able-bodied raced to pull trapped survivors from the wreckage before the fires could reach them. One of the passengers, Henry Tewksbury, found himself pinned to his seat. He could only watch as the fire approached. Tewksbury must have cursed his luck. He wasn't even supposed to be on that train. He was traveling home to Randolph, but had planned to stay overnight in White River. The town, however, had only one hotel and it was full. So, despite the late hour, he had decided to take what should have been a thirty-minute ride home.

Now he lay trapped between fire and ice.

"It was a time of mental torture," he later recalled, "but I still could not help noticing an old couple who had sat a few seats behind me. They were hopelessly tied down by heavy seats, and the flames were approaching them with frightful rapidity. I could do nothing for them. Before the smoke shut them from sight, I saw them locked in each other's arms."

Tewksbury was sure the fire would take him next. He couldn't stand to watch, so he pulled his fur hat over his eyes "to hide the dreadful view of approaching death."

At that moment, he heard voices of rescuers and called for help. "Two powerful men," he said, strained to pull him from the wreckage. But he was stuck fast. The men considered giving up, not wanting to waste time when others could be saved, but Tewksbury pleaded with them.

"I begged them to try once more—to pull my leg off if they had to, but not let me burn," he said. "They pulled—and, oh, with what a joyous feeling did I feel my feet gradually slipping from my shoes. I cried out that I was moving—to pull, pull, pull! I felt one of my legs break, but I was released."

In their haste, the men nearly left him beside the burning cars, but he persuaded them to place him somewhere safer, leaning against one of the bridge's stone supports.

The rescuers were apparently mostly crew members who had been on the two cars that had been spared. Most of the people on the derailed cars had either been killed or were too badly hurt to help.

Rescuers spotted Sturtevant, the conductor, crawling through a train car, the back of his clothes on fire. Trying desperately to help, the rescuers could only shovel snow at him through a broken window. By the time the fire was extinguished and he was pulled from the wreckage, Sturtevant was in bad shape. His comrades carried him gingerly to the farmhouse of Oscar Paine, which sat at the north end of the bridge. There the conductor died several hours later.

Tewksbury, who by now realized he had also broken an arm, watched the men carry Sturtevant away. He yelled to them that he would need their help when they returned. He needed moving again. Fire from the train cars had ignited the wooden bridge above him. The top of the bridge had been built with iron sheeting along its entire length to prevent sparks from a passing train starting a fire. Understandably, no one had imagined that the fire could come from the river below.

Rescuers managed to return in time to carry Tewksbury to the Paine farmhouse before the bridge collapsed.

We'll never know exactly how many of the eighty-nine people aboard the train died that night. Accounts of the wreck list the number as anywhere from thirty to thirty-nine. The grim job of counting the dead was made harder by the devastating fire, which left nothing on the ice that resembled a train except for steel wheels and axles. Some accounts don't even attempt to put a number on the tragedy, listing the number simply as "many."

TEDDY LEARNS
McKINLEY'S BEEN SHOT

1901

THEODORE ROOSEVELT WAS THE MAN OF THE HOUR. Roughly one thousand people turned out on September 6, 1901, to catch a glimpse of him and hear him speak. Roosevelt had gained national attention for bravely leading his Rough Riders at the Battle of San Juan Hill during the recent Spanish-American War, and now he was vice president.

But events unfolding nearly four hundred miles away would overshadow anything Roosevelt had to say that day. People who heard him speak soon cared little about what he had said; they were focused instead on what he might soon become.

Roosevelt had been touring the state, having made stops in Rutland and Burlington. Now he was attending the Vermont Fish and Game League's annual dinner at the home of former lieutenant governor Nelson W. Fisk in Isle LaMotte. Despite its name, the league wasn't concerned with wildlife so much as with politics. Roosevelt was in town to check in with political allies and lend gravitas to the event, just as President William McKinley had four years earlier.

Hundreds of visitors reached Isle LaMotte aboard the *Chateaugay* steamship and other smaller boats, tying up at Fisk's dock. At about 1:30 p.m., the guest of honor and about one thousand others sat down for dinner and speeches under a massive tent on Fisk's lakeside property. The most memorable may have been delivered by Jeremiah Curtin, a noted folklorist and linguist, who was said to be proficient in seventy languages. Curtin later wrote in his memoirs that he had not expected to speak that day, but when he was called on by the emcee to make a few remarks, he was not at a loss for words.

"This is a feast at which the host is a great state, represented by its leading citizens," Curtin said. "The guest of honor is the most widely known, public man in America; the man most intimately known by the people; the heir at law of the White House—and millions of American citizens hope that in the future he will be the occupant of that mansion."

Curtin couldn't have realized how soon his words would become true.

After the dinner, Roosevelt returned to Fisk's house to rest briefly before hosting a reception that evening. But that event would soon be canceled.

At 5:30 p.m., Fisk's phone rang. It was for Roosevelt. The caller, whose name has apparently been lost to history, reported hearing a rumor that the president had been shot. Moments later a second call confirmed the report. Less than an hour and a half earlier, McKinley had been shot twice during a reception at the Pan-American Exposition in Buffalo.

John Barrett, former U.S. minister to Siam, was in Fisk's home when Roosevelt got the news. "He was changing his clothes when called to the telephone," Barrett told the *New York Times*. "As soon as he realized the meaning of the terrible news, a dazed expression followed by a look of unmistakable anguish came to his face, and tears immediately filled his eyes: He was plainly laboring under deep emotion, and asked [Vermont] Senator [Redfield] Proctor, likewise keenly affected, to make the sad announcement to the waiting crowd."

Proctor dutifully went outside and, after quieting the crowd, said, "Friends, a cloud has fallen over this happy event. It is my sad duty to inform you that President McKinley, while in the Temple of Music at Buffalo, was this afternoon shot twice by an anarchist, two bullets having taken effect. His condition is said to be serious, but we hope that later intelligence may prove the statement to be exaggerated."

With the announcement, the *Vermonter* magazine reported in its November 1901 edition, "a moan of sorrow went up from the entire assemblage and many burst into tears."

Soon, Roosevelt received word that doctors believed McKinley might survive.

"[T]he vice president exclaimed with sincerest feeling: 'That's good—it is good. May it be every bit true,' " Barrett recalled, "and immediately he brushed aside those about him, hastened out on the veranda, and made the reassuring announcement himself."

Despite the encouraging report, Roosevelt decided he should be with the president. Dr. W. Seward Webb, the owner of Shelburne Farms, offered to take the vice president to Burlington aboard his yacht, *Elfrida*. En route, someone mentioned to Roosevelt that he might arrive in Burlington to the news that he was president. "Do not speak of that contingency," Roosevelt responded, according to Barrett. "Our one thought and prayer is now for the president, and that he may be spared."

When the *Elfrida* docked in Burlington, McKinley was still alive. And for a time, it seemed he might survive the attempt on his life. By September 12, he had regained enough strength to eat solid foods, a hopeful sign. But later that day, his condition quickly worsened. Two days later, President McKinley died from gangrene that had developed around his wounds. Jeremiah Curtin's offhand remark about Roosevelt's future in the White House had proved prophetic.

THE JAILING OF A MINISTER

1917

IF CLARENCE WALDRON EVER WONDERED whether he was in trouble, the crowd must have removed any doubts. A throng of people—estimates range from three hundred to one thousand—swarmed around him at his place of work, demanding he defend what he had done, or rather hadn't done, earlier that day. Waldron bravely met the crowd on the steps of the First Baptist Church of Windsor, where he was minister, and tried to explain. It wouldn't be easy—not to this crowd, not in this era.

It was October 21, 1917, and America was in a war frenzy. The country had joined the fighting in the Great War six months earlier, and bodies of American boys were returning home from battlefields overseas.

People were so concerned about the war that some even feared the fighting would reach America's shores. Some Vermonters around White River Junction armed themselves and took turns guarding railroad bridges against German saboteurs.

If any Vermont community was going to support the war aggressively, it would be Windsor. When fighting erupted in Europe in 1914, the local machine tool industry kicked into high gear to meet the orders that flowed from the warring nations. As workers streamed into town to fill factory jobs, Windsor's population doubled.

The day Waldron faced the crowd was the date that President Woodrow Wilson had designated "Liberty Loan Sunday," when he expected the nation's clergy to decorate their churches in red, white, and blue and to lead their congregations in singing "The Star-Spangled Banner." The idea was to encourage congregants to buy Liberty Bonds to fund the war.

Across the country, clergy members complied. So too in Windsor, except at Waldron's church, where that Sunday's service was no different than usual. Word of Waldron's decision spread quickly, and by evening the crowd had gathered outside his church.

His patriotism clearly questioned, Waldron responded by saying that he was "as loyal an American as ever walked in shoe leather." His family was American through and through, he insisted, and could trace its roots to the *Mayflower*. Waldron said he supported his government and deplored the German Kaiser. His opposition to selling war bonds in church wasn't political, but religious. He said that as a minister he found it wrong to discuss earthly matters in church. He apparently didn't mention it, but his religious beliefs had long ago made him a pacifist.

Under pressure from the crowd to prove his patriotism, Waldron wrapped himself in the American flag and sang "The Star-Spangled Banner," accompanied by his wife and some friends from his congregation.

Clarence Waldron's fight to defend his name might have been forgotten if not for the research of historian Gene Sessions, professor emeritus of history from Norwich University.

Waldron had studied at an evangelical Bible school with a Pentecostal bent and been ordained a Baptist minister before landing the job in Windsor in 1915. Emulating the flashy, charismatic style of famed evangelist Billy Sunday, Waldron soon roughly tripled the number who attended church each Sunday. He seemed more a pillar of the community than an enemy of the state.

But, Sessions says, Waldron had made enemies in making converts. He had noticed a street-corner Pentecostal preacher in town who was especially good at drawing crowds. The man did this by "healing the sick, casting out demons, and speaking in other languages as the Spirit gives utterance," as an advertisement in a local newspaper promised. Waldron soon decided to conduct similar services, and eventually the Pentecostals began attending his Baptist church. But a rift developed. Longtime members objected to the presence of Pentecostals and their flamboyant displays of faith.

Several days after the dispute on the church steps, members of Waldron's congregation asked him to resign. The issue was the Pentecostals, though the war-bonds controversy may have lurked in the background. The minister refused to quit.

Next, the church's organizing group, the Vermont Baptist State Convention, began pressuring Waldron to resign. He retorted that "Pentecostal truth" and "Baptist truth" were both "God's unchanging truth" and again refused to resign, saying that Windsor was primed for "a real religious awakening." The board, unmoved, fired him.

Denied a church, Waldron continued to conduct Pentecostal meetings at his home. If he thought his troubles were over, he was wrong. Almost immediately after his firing, a federal grand jury in Brattleboro began investigating him for antiwar activities. The grand jury indicted Waldron for violating the Espionage Act just passed by Congress. Despite the name, the act contained a section that had nothing to do with spying. The act called for prison terms of up to twenty years to "whoever, when the United States is at war, . . . shall willfully obstruct the recruiting or enlistment service of the U.S. . . ."

Parishioners accused him of making unpatriotic statements in church and in private, and of trying to dissuade young men from enlisting. He had allegedly told men in a Bible class that a Christian shouldn't fight, and distributed a pamphlet that reiterated the argument. Furthermore, he had once been heard to say "to hell with patriotism."

When he took the stand, Waldron acknowledged that he believed Christians should not fight wars. The Ten Commandments forbade killing, he explained. Ironically, he had distributed the pamphlet in hopes of calming tensions after the church-step controversy.

On the stand, he also admitted making the comment about patriotism, but explained that he had made it before the United States entered the war. And the comment had been about the extreme German nationalism that had sparked the conflict. "If this is patriotism," he had said, "to hell with patriotism."

The jury, perhaps perceiving that a religious dispute was part of Waldron's troubles, failed to reach a verdict. During a second trial, at which the judge barred any testimony related to the dispute, the jury convicted Waldron. The judge sentenced him to fifteen years in prison.

Waldron never completed his sentence. A year after entering prison, with the war having ended months earlier, President Wilson pardoned him and many others convicted under the Espionage Act. Waldron assumed a Pentecostal ministry and settled, with his wife and daughter, far from Vermont.

THE FAMOUS ICE FLOE SCENE

1920

THE MOVIE IS LONG FORGOTTEN, but the scene is well remembered. It is a classic of the silent-movie era. A young woman lies unconscious on an ice floe as it floats downriver toward a waterfall. All the while, her lover braves the teetering ice sheets, desperately trying to reach her.

The scene, from D. W. Griffith's 1920 movie *Way Down East*, was shot in White River Junction. The actor trying to save the heroine was a junior at nearby Dartmouth College. But the star was a young actress named Lillian Gish, who was already a matinee idol and would continue acting for nearly another seventy years.

Though she appeared in scores of movies, and lived to the age of ninety-nine, Gish never forgot her time in Vermont. Perhaps it was the hardships she faced in creating the famous scene and the emotional reaction it elicited from audience members at screenings.

Gish and the rest of Griffith's company descended on White River Junction in March 1920 to shoot the ice scenes for *Way Down East*. The winter had been short on snow, so the company had spent the time filming indoor scenes at Griffith's studio in Mamaroneck, New York. To prepare for the grueling outdoor scenes that awaited, Gish regularly took cold baths. When a snowstorm hit Vermont, Gish and the rest of the company packed their bags and headed north.

In *Way Down East,* Gish plays a young woman named Anna Moore who is wooed by a city playboy, who tricks her by pretending to marry her. When she becomes pregnant, he deserts her. The unwed mother gives birth, but the child dies. (This isn't a particularly cheery movie, until the end.) She finds work on a farm and falls in love with the farmer's son, played by Dartmouth student Dick Barthelmess. But the playboy owns the farm next door, so word reaches the farmer about Anna's pregnancy. Morally outraged, and misinformed about the details of Anna's past, the farmer casts the poor woman out of his house, and into the teeth of a driving blizzard. Anna tries to cross the river, but faints on the ice, which promptly breaks off. The ice sheet she is lying on floats downriver, toward the waterfall. But the farmer's son has learned what his father has done and is chasing after Gish. Braving the shifting ice floes, he snatches her up just before the ice sheet slips over the falls.

The scenes were shot mostly without stand-ins. But one local woman, Rachel Gordon, whose handwritten recollections of the filming are at the Vermont Historical Society, remembered that a stand-in for Gish fell into the freezing White River. She was scooped out, taken to a nearby house, stripped of her clothes, and wrapped in blankets. A doctor arrived and gave her medicine in hopes of warding off pneumonia, then she was put to bed for several days before she was allowed to return to her hotel.

For the three weeks of shooting in White River, Gish risked a similar dunking. She had to venture onto the bobbing ice for about twenty takes a day. "I had the bright idea to have my hand and hair trail in the water," she recalled a half century after the film was shot. "I thought it would be more realistic having the girl swoon from exhaustion. Of course, once I had my hand in that ice-cold water in front of the camera, I couldn't remove it. It still aches today when it gets cold."

The weather was bitter cold during filming. The temperature was stuck below zero. The cameraman had to set a fire beneath the camera to keep the lens from icing over. At least the filmmakers didn't have to worry about the ice being too thin to hold Gish.

They had another problem, though. The river was frozen solid, so if they wanted ice floes, they would have to make them. Workers used saws to break off sections of ice. Sometimes they resorted to using dynamite. The sections were then held in place by ropes and only released on the director's word. For some shots, Griffith ordered a cameraman to accompany Gish on her ice floe, so he could get another angle.

Townspeople crowded around to watch the filming. They don't seem to have caused any problems for Griffith, though. The same wasn't true when they decided to film parts of the river scene on the Connecticut River near the Wilder Dam. Dartmouth students turned out to heckle their fellow student, Barthelmess, during filming. "Shut up!" Griffith barked at them. (Fortunately, it was a silent movie.) When the taunts distracted Barthelmess, Griffith advised him, "Don't pay any attention to those savages."

Making the movie wasn't all cold, hard work, however. The actors stayed at the comfortable Junction House (now the Hotel Coolidge) in White River Junction. Evenings, after dinner in the large dining room, the tables would be moved away and a fiddler brought in to perform. Cast members, as well as members of the hotel staff and assorted guests, would then take part in a square dance. It wasn't just for fun, though. Griffith wanted his actors to learn how to do square dances for a scene they would shoot later. The hotel's manager, Nathaniel Wheeler, even arranged for cast members to attend a barn dance nearby.

Wheeler also plied the actors with maple syrup, which he procured from a sugar maker in Quechee. And when the sap began to flow, Rachel Gordon wrote in her reminiscences, her husband invited actors to a sugaring off party, where they had what, for most of them, must have been their first taste of sugar-on-snow, complete with plain donuts and pickles to cut the sweetness. The warm treatment must have been almost enough for the actors to forget the brutally cold conditions they would face during the next day's filming.

Shooting ended as spring arrived. The actors left, perhaps wondering whether their efforts in Vermont had been worth it. They needn't have worried. *Way Down East* was a hit—and the icy river scene is the most memorable scene. Because of the pains Gish went through, the scene seemed real to people—perhaps too real for some. Years later, Gish explained people's reactions to the scene: "So many people fainted that Mr. Griffith had a trained nurse in the ladies' room," she said. "But he didn't want word to get out about the fainting. It would have been bad for business."

COOLIDGE'S SUMMER WHITE HOUSE

1924

FOR THREE AND A HALF HOURS on the morning of August 16, 1924, the president of the United States slept in a train car sitting on a railway siding in Ludlow. Calvin Coolidge was returning to his boyhood home in nearby Plymouth for two weeks of rest to escape the heat and pressures of Washington.

It was Coolidge's third visit to Plymouth in the last year. He surely hoped this one would not be surrounded by tragedy. During the first trip, in August 1923, Coolidge, then the vice president, had been awakened by his father, who told him that Warren G. Harding had died and he was now president. Coolidge had returned eleven months later to bury his younger son, Calvin Jr., who had died at the age of sixteen of blood poisoning after a blister became infected.

Coolidge, his wife, Grace, and son, John, woke early that morning in Ludlow, ate breakfast, then were driven to Plymouth. They traveled at twenty miles per hour, which one newspaper reported was the president's preferred rate of speed. With them was a phalanx of Secret Service agents and journalists. When they arrived at the village, only about fifty people had turned out to witness the president's arrival. Vermonters were seemingly caught off guard by his early-morning arrival, though newspapers had announced his general travel plans. Over the coming days, however, people from across the state and region would flock to Plymouth. The peace the president sought would only be preserved by the distance imposed by Secret Service agents.

The Coolidges stayed with the president's father, John, whose house was just down the road from Florence Cilley's General Store. Fifty-two years earlier, Coolidge had been born in a house attached to that store. Now a meeting hall above the store was serving as his presidential office.

When reporters asked Coolidge's secretary, C. Bascom Slemp, what the president's plans were for his first days of vacation, he could provide few details. The president wanted to relax and visit with family and old friends, Slemp said. Coolidge could stay in touch with Washington, though, telephone and telegraph lines having been strung to the meeting hall.

Despite the growing crowds, the Secret Service and state and county officials managed to keep order. A reporter for the *Barre Times* described how upon entering the village, a driver "is passed along by a beautiful system of handling until he finds himself and car parked in one of the pastures lining the little village." There wasn't much to see in Plymouth, the reporter noted, just a few houses and the general store, "unless one happens to turn his eyes sharply to the right, there to see a set of buildings up the street and a little church just opposite. This set of buildings up the street is the temporary White House of the country."

The Coolidges attended services at the church on Sunday, August 17. A couple hundred people packed the building to join them. Afterward, the Coolidges strolled to their temporary residence, while visitors flocked to the general store and just-opened tearoom and souvenir shop to buy postcards and other mementos.

Coolidge tried to make life as normal as possible, reading or visiting with guests. Edward Blanchard, who owned a farm next to John Coolidge's place, mentioned that he'd had trouble harvesting crops due to family illness. The president, who was free the next afternoon, volunteered to help. Coolidge often did chores when visiting Plymouth, which probably reminded him of his childhood. But rain scrubbed the plans.

Despite the normalcy Coolidge sought, he was living in a fishbowl. Secret Service agents set up a "dead line" ten yards from the house, across which no one could cross without permission. Reporters for the news wire services were among those toeing the line. From them, Americans learned of the president's latest activities, which, since this was a vacation, were limited. The public read that he huddled with Charles Dawes, his running mate in the upcoming fall elections; that he received briefings on the successful renegotiation of Germany's reparations for its role in the Great War; and that he entertained inventors Thomas Edison and Henry Ford and tire magnate Harvey Firestone—the three recently having become traveling companions.

But the public wanted to know more, reported the *Brattleboro Reformer*. "A lot of people outside of Vermont are going to be disappointed if the newspaper men cannot report sometime during the next week or so that the president ate pie for breakfast," the paper joked, eating pie at breakfast being considered the mark of a true Yankee.

Advisors suggested the president host a large field day–style event, "with half the people of the state present as a tribute to their distinguished fellow-citizen," the *Rutland Herald* reported, "but the quiet executive kibosh was placed on the publicity plan, just as several other similar plans were in the same fashion dropped at a word from him."

Instead, Coolidge and his wife would host a simple public reception on his father's lawn. The event opened the floodgates. To accommodate the anticipated crowds, the state Highway Patrol made the road from West Bridgewater to Plymouth Union one-way during the hours leading up to the event, then reversed the direction for the hours afterward.

Thousands of cars poured down the little road and parked in fields surrounding the village. An estimated ten thousand to twenty thousand people waited their turn to shake hands with the president and first lady. "For two hours," the *Vermont Standard* newspaper of Woodstock wrote, "the people continued to pass by to speak their carefully rehearsed words of greeting." And afterward, they lingered as long as they could to watch "a scene as they knew they were not likely to see again."

"The patriarchs of the State came to Plymouth," the *Standard* reported. "The little children from miles around were brought up by their parents to tell their grandchildren some day of the time when they shook hands with Vermont's president, Calvin Coolidge and his wife."

THE GREAT FLOOD

1927

THE FIRST SIGN OF TROUBLE WENT UNHEEDED. What was a little water in the basement? Since it had rained nearly every day for the last month, it was to be expected. Why should today be more dangerous?

It was at midday, November 3, 1927, when some merchants in Barre noticed water rising in their basements. Others who lived and worked along the Winooski River and its tributaries were making similar discoveries. Gerald Brock and Ralph Winter, employees at a hardware store on Barre's Main Street, went downstairs with two others to save merchandise in the neighboring clothing store. Unknown to the four, the basement of an adjoining building had already filled with water from an overflowing brook. The wall separating the basements suddenly burst. Two men ran or were pulled up the stairs. Brock and Winter drowned. They were Barre's first flood deaths that day.

Another eighty-two people across Vermont, including Vermont's lieutenant governor, Hollister Jackson, were killed. Fifteen people would die when their boardinghouse was swept over Bolton Falls on the Winooski—the deadliest river to live near on that fateful day.

Despite all the rain, the flood actually came as a surprise. The forecast had called for fair weather; but a tropical storm working its way up the East Coast unexpectedly veered inland and met a rainstorm coming from the west. As a result, rain fell on the night of November 2—and continued for thirty-eight hours.

When the Winooski escaped its banks, people had little time to escape. At times, the waters were rising four feet an hour. Among those caught off guard was Frank Dawley, a former mayor of Montpelier. Dawley found himself trapped in his workshop. As the waters climbed, the seventy-seven-year-old climbed too: first onto the counters and then up the shelves that he had along one wall. There, for twelve hours, he was able to hold his head just above the swirling water. Percy Bailey, janitor at the First National Bank in Montpelier, saved himself by holding onto some molding near the ceiling of the counting room for eighteen hours.

Not everyone was so fortunate.

The Walter Sargent family of Waterbury were trapped in their home, which was in danger of breaking loose from its foundation. Firemen tried to reach the family, but the fast current made rescue impossible. Witnesses saw Sargent trying desperately to get the family cow up to the second floor. The house abruptly rose in the water, and drifted quickly away, disintegrating as it struck obstacles, and killing Sargent, his wife, four children, and mother-in-law.

Trying to escape could prove equally dangerous. The Harry Cutting family of Waterbury fled their house when the water reached the second floor. Harry fashioned a raft from a pair of doors. His wife, Gladys, climbed aboard with their three children, ages 2, 4, and 6. As they were paddling for higher ground, a large object struck the raft, capsizing it. Gladys and the children drowned. Harry Cutting managed to grab onto a tree, from which rescuers plucked him twelve hours later.

A group of laborers and their families in Barre were trapped in thirteen neighboring story-and-a-half houses. Word of their plight reached rescuers about 6:00 p.m. on November 3. The water was moving so quickly that firemen, Vermont National Guard members, and other volunteers decided the only way to reach the houses was by stretching sixty-foot ladders over the torrent. They lit the scene with car headlights and lay down the first ladder. They reached one house and then repeated the process to reach the next. "The people were terror-stricken," remembered fireman John Anderson, "as they faced the choice of remaining in their homes, likely to be washed away any moment, or of making the perilous trip over the shaky and bending ladders, only a few inches above the raging current."

Word spread that Lieutenant Governor Jackson was missing. Jackson had gotten his car stuck in a gully that the flood had carved through the road. Witnesses saw him stumble through the driving rain, trying to walk home. All night, his car sat in the washout, its lights on. His body was discovered the next morning.

In desperate straits, Vermonters proved themselves resourceful. Trapped with his family and twelve others, undertaker V. L. Perkins used what he had on hand. He nailed together a pair of coffins and used them to ferry people to safety.

Mrs. George Buswell of Montpelier was stuck in her attic with her nine children. Through the night, Mrs. Buswell played records on her Victrola to distract the children from the frightening noises outside, where uprooted trees, livestock, even houses were streaming through the neighborhood.

The next day, when the flooding began to subside, Vermonters started to assess the damage. Eventually, the losses would be counted at $30 million, then a tremendous amount of money. But it was surely the images that stuck with people—the dead bodies, the dirt everywhere, the miles of roads and railroad tracks washed away, the vacant lots where houses once stood.

One Montpelier resident returned home to find a dead pony lodged under his piano. Another found a pig swimming down his hallway.

Perhaps the grimmest task was left to people in Middlesex, where the flood had washed away part of a cemetery, taking with it fourteen caskets. Many of the caskets opened as they were pulled toward Montpelier by the floodwaters. Seven of the bodies were never recovered.

As they rebuilt their towns and their lives, Vermonters couldn't shake the memories. Writer Luther Johnson described the terrifying sights Vermonters had witnessed in his 1928 book *Vermont in Floodtime*.

Everything that could float, including articles of great bulk and weight, came bobbing or tumbling along. Now and then a huge building or part of a bridge would rush out of the darkness with the speed and force of a locomotive and disappear in a moment.

Constantly there was the apprehension of some hapless human being beyond the reach of aid gliding along to a water grave. And the roar of the monster was terrifying, never to be forgotten, incessant, so deafening that people tried unavailingly to close their ears to it.

THE DEFEAT OF THE GREEN
MOUNTAIN PARKWAY

1935

COLONEL WILLIAM WILGUS MUST HAVE ENVISIONED IT as the ambitious project that would cap his illustrious career. As a civil engineer, Wilgus had helped design the new Grand Central Terminal and Holland Tunnel in New York City, had run the U.S. Army transportation service in France during the Great War, and had even righted some of the columns of the Parthenon in Athens.

Now, having retired to Vermont, Wilgus looked out at the Green Mountains and imagined a highway running along their flanks and peaks. In his vision, this road, soon to be dubbed the Green Mountain Parkway, would cover 260 miles, from the Massachusetts line to the Canadian border. It would employ thousands of Vermonters who had been left jobless by the Depression, bring countless visitors to the state, and, best of all, would cost Vermont almost nothing. This was the 1930s and the New Deal, the federal government's economic recovery plan, was spending millions on public works programs.

The project seemed unstoppable. Vermont's share of the $18 million project would be a scant $500,000. The state would spend that money to buy rights-of-way along the route, then deed the land to the federal government for a national park.

Wilgus had influential allies, among them legislative leaders, former governors, and famed author Dorothy Canfield Fisher of Arlington. Most importantly, he had an indefatigable ally in James P. Taylor, father of the Long Trail and founder of the Green Mountain Club. His backing would blunt claims that the road would despoil Vermont.

Taylor, however, was not a hard-core environmentalist. He would promote anything he thought would increase Vermont's vitality. After helping found the Green Mountain Club, he had joined the Greater Vermont Association, forerunner of the state Chamber of Commerce. Taylor was equally enthusiastic about trails and roads.

Also promoting the highway were newspapers in northern and central Vermont. The *Burlington Free Press* editorialized strongly in favor of the road. And, according to Taylor's notes, the *Waterbury Record* wrote in August 1933 that "when a man of the experience [and] knowledge that [the] Colonel possesses figures that it is a good thing for Vermont to do . . . it just behooves the average person to fall into line."

The parkway also had many enemies. Chief among them was the Green Mountain Club itself. In 1933, GMC trustees declared the organization "unalterably opposed to the construction of such a highway." The parkway "would commercialize a section of the State that has so far been unspoiled."

If an environmental argument wouldn't sway everyone, trustees suggested that maintenance of the parkway could become a financial burden to the state. Among the club's most influential members were Representative Mortimer Proctor (soon to be Speaker of the House and later governor) and Henry Field, publisher of the *Rutland Herald,* the most state's influential paper at the time.

The parkway's opponents worried that the road would draw tourists away from the villages, which needed their business, and attract a "flood of undesirable visitors." A distrust of outsiders united some opponents. Here, after all, was a pair of nonnative Vermonters (Wilgus and Taylor were both from upstate New York) inviting the federal government in to make mischief. Also, the parkway would physically divide the state east and west as it had always been divided politically.

Supporters, for their part, couldn't understand why opponents would reject the blessings of modernity and the economic benefits this state-of-the-art parkway would bring. Wilgus assured Vermonters that the road's landscaping and layout would shield it from the eyes and ears of hikers. He also attacked those who worried about "undesirable visitors." "As if we wished to remain a 'hermit kingdom' for all time," Wilgus wrote emphatically, "just because an occasional visitor via the parkway may not be all that is to be desired." Privately, he called people who worried about newcomers "snobs."

By 1934, supporters seemed to have the upper hand. The state and federal government acted as if the project had already been approved. A team of surveyors, engineers, and architects began laying out a route running along Glastonbury Mountain, Killington Peak, Camel's Hump, and Mount Mansfield before ending at the Canadian border.

Even GMC's trustees began to view the parkway as inevitable and worked to minimize its impact. The club proposed running the parkway through the state's valleys to protect the mountains and keep visitors in the villages, where their business was needed.

The Legislature voted on the Green Mountain Parkway in early 1935. The proposal easily passed the Senate, 19 to 11. But supporters were stunned when the House narrowly defeated it, 126 to 111. Wilgus was stung. He wrote Taylor that summer: "It is really too bad that Vermonters have so deliberately turned their back on their great opportunity."

Taylor wrote back, offering Wilgus hope: "Well, it's a process to which we are more or less accustomed, this mental measles before projects are accepted here in Vermont as well as everywhere else. It took years to sell the Long Trail idea some places in Vermont."

The vote was so tight, and feelings so intense on both sides, that the Legislature ultimately decided to put the parkway's fate before the people. Under the state Constitution, only the Legislature can set law, but it can look to the public for advice. So in a special session, legislators approved funding for the parkway with two enactment dates—one in 1936, the other in 1941.

It was essentially a yes-no vote on the highway. If people picked 1936, the road was a go. If they chose 1941, lawmakers promised to repeal the funding. On Town Meeting Day 1936, Vermont-ers finally got a chance to weigh in on the debate. In droves, they crowded their town halls to vote. They were far less divided than their representatives, defeating the parkway 42,318 to 30,897, or by a margin of 58 percent to 42.

Politicians and scholars have debated the meaning of the vote ever since. It was the victory of southern Vermonters, who feared tourists would zoom right past them, over northern Vermonters, who thought they'd snare that business. Or, others argued, it was the defeat of capitalists by conservationists; or native Vermont con-servatism winning out over the big, federal government. Whatever it signified, the public's vote meant one thing for sure: The Green Mountain Parkway was dead.

THE CAMEL'S HUMP CRASH

1944

THE MEN WERE COLD. Outside the airplane, the temperature was about 5 degrees. Inside, it was no warmer. To take the chill off, the pilot used an old aviation trick. He dropped the plane from the standard training altitude of eight thousand feet to four thousand feet, thereby raising the temperature inside about 12 degrees. It seemed a safe enough maneuver. Nothing in their flight path was above four thousand feet.

The men were in the home stretch of a three-hour training mission during World War II. Most of them stayed in their seats, huddled over their instruments. One, the top turret gunner, wandered into the tail section to nap. It was almost 1:00 a.m. Slowly, imperceptibly, the plane strayed from its intended path.

As the plane cruised above the Vermont countryside, perhaps they found time to chat briefly about what they'd do next time they got leave. Perhaps they glanced out the windows to check their bearings. Not much to see, though. It was a moonless night, and the homes in the valley below were blacked out. There is no way they could see the mountain looming dead ahead.

What happened in the hours ahead was only pieced together recently, thanks to the tireless research of Brian Lindner, an insurance executive and part-time historian. Linder first learned of the crash in 1963 while climbing Camel's Hump at the age of eleven. Growing up in the Waterbury-Stowe area, he had somehow missed the local legend of the bomber crash. But he came face to face with it that day while climbing the 4,083-foot-high peak. As he walked among the stunted trees huddled below the mountain's south face, he suddenly caught a glimpse of a huge silvery wing.

"I was just fascinated by it," recalls Lindner. Discovering the remains of an airplane on a mountainside was bizarre enough, but the explanations he got of what happened there were stranger still. He heard various stories: It was a cargo plane, it was a Nazi spy plane; no, it was a B-52. None of the answers made sense.

"Even at age eleven, I said this can't be true," he says. "There has got to be more to this." In the years since that day, he managed to uncover the story, which had gotten lost among all the other tragedies of World War II.

The plane, a B-24 Liberator, had taken off on an October night in 1944 from Westover Field in Chicopee, Massachusetts, and had flown for several hours before somehow colliding with Camel's Hump, killing nine crew members instantly. Miraculously, the tenth, the napping gunner, survived. The temperature dropped into the low 20s as Jimmy Wilson lay unconscious, cocooned inside the tail section of the smashed plane. The rest of the airplane was shattered and scattered across the snowy flank of the mountain. The search for survivors wouldn't start until morning.

At first light, military and Civil Air Patrol personnel throughout the Northeast began the hunt. They knew the procedure; this was an all-to-familiar task. Westover Field alone had lost three bombers on training missions in recent months. Search planes scoured the hills and valleys around Burlington, the B-24's last-known position. Low cloud cover prevented them from searching mountaintops. When the clouds finally lifted on the second day, the crew of an army airplane spotted the crash site on the southeast corner of the mountain at 2:30 p.m.

Someone, however, made a mistake plotting the site's map coordinates, and the army dispatched a search party to the mountain's west side. Major William Mason, director of Civil Air Patrol operations in Vermont, caught the error and tried to explain it to the army captain directing the search, but the captain dismissed the claim. So Mason called his son, Peter, a senior at Waterbury High School, and told him to gather other Civil Air Patrol cadets at the school to search the mountain. They were determined to find the plane, even if the army couldn't.

Seven young cadets, accompanied by a local doctor and two other men, raced up a steep trail toward the summit in the fading daylight. Even if survivors had somehow endured two cold nights on the mountain, they might not survive a third. The sun set, but the cadets kept searching. They figured they must be close. Finally, in the growing gloom, they stumbled into a scene of devastation. Splintered trees and airplane parts lay strewn across the hillside. The air reeked of aviation fuel. Then they heard a noise, a voice, and frantically scurried down a steep embankment to find it. In seconds, they came upon the remains of the fuselage. And there, lying dazed against it, was Jimmy Wilson.

Wilson's ordeal was only beginning when rescuers found him. As he was recovering in the hospital, a doctor told him matter-of-factly that he'd lose his hands and feet to frostbite. The doctor said, "You're never going to amount to anything, just get used to the idea." Wilson lay in his bed and cried. Then he realized what he had to do. "I decided to prove the S.O.B. wrong," he later told Lindner, who had tracked him down. After leaving the hospital, Wilson managed to graduate from college and law school, become an attorney, marry, and raise a family.

Lindner admired Wilson for his grit and humor. When they first met, Wilson greeted Lindner by offering one of his metal hooks to shake. It was Wilson's way of saying his handicap was no big deal. Besides, having hooks wasn't that bad, he told Lindner, jokingly; they meant you never had to buy potholders.

Despite his obsession with the crash, Lindner has not forgotten that the story is even more important for another group of people, the relatives of the crew members. His research provided answers they had waited decades to hear. "The families never knew what happened," he says. "They got four telegrams. They got one saying your son or husband is missing. They got a second telegram saying the bomber he was on has been found; rescue operations are in progress. A third telegram saying your son or husband is dead. And another telegram saying his body is coming home." The army had few other details to offer. In the midst of World War II, the army had little time to investigate.

Lindner met many of the relatives, including the mothers of two of the victims, at a ceremony marking the forty-fifth anniversary of the crash. When local veterans dedicated a plaque to the men at the base of the mountain where they died, the mothers cried.

"Many people can tell you that World War II ended in 1945," Lindner says. "But having met these families, and particularly the mothers of these crewmen, I can now say that World War II isn't over until the last close relative of these guys is dead."

Maybe Lindner should include himself among the mourners. The B-24 crashed long ago, but Lindner still feels the tragic weight of it. Perhaps heaviest to bear is that Lindner knows how close the accident came to *not* happening. In his research, he determined that the plane nicked Camel's Hump with the very tip of its left wing. "If they'd been eighteen inches to the right, they would have gone right by it and never known," Lindner says. "There is nothing else that high in front of them the rest of the way."

THE NOVIKOFF FIRING

1953

HIS DAYS AT THE UNIVERSITY OF VERMONT WERE NUMBERED: Professor Alex Novikoff knew that much. He had worked hard to get there and was now, in 1953, a highly respected cancer researcher. But the school's board of trustees had given him an ultimatum: Either name former colleagues who had had Communist sympathies, or pack his things. Either talk or walk. Novikoff knew what his answer had to be.

Novikoff was in hot water because of testimony he had given to a Senate panel earlier that year. He said he would speak freely of his days since joining the UVM faculty in 1948 and taking the school's required loyalty oath. "I am not a Communist," he told the committee chaired by Senator William Jenner of Indiana. But when senators asked questions about events before that date, Novikoff declined to answer, citing his Fifth Amendment rights to remain silent.

Novikoff's silence drew a loud response in Vermont. Newspapers across the state ran stories on his testimony before the committee. The *Burlington Free Press* ran a story under the headline: "UVM Professor Balks at Jenner Red Quiz."

What Novikoff was unwilling to discuss was that in 1935, while a graduate student at Columbia University and an instructor at Brooklyn College, he had joined the Communist Party. Like many leftists of the day, he was drawn to the movement by idealism. He had supported many progressive causes on campus, including fighting for faculty members' right to form a union. Later, disillusioned with the Soviet Union and fearful of what involvement with Communists might do to his career, Novikoff quit the party.

Now, with Senator Joseph McCarthy leading the cold war effort to ferret out Communists in America, Novikoff's past began to take on a more sinister air. He wasn't helped by the fact he had been born in Russia and emigrated as an infant to the United States.

UVM president Carl Borgmann had come under intense pressure to review Novikoff's appointment at the university, including from Governor Lee Emerson, who by virtue of his office was an ex-officio member of the UVM board. Novikoff had been granted tenure—technically a lifetime appointment that is supposed to encourage academic freedom—but the university claimed the right to revoke it.

Borgmann appointed a committee to review Novikoff's actions and make a recommendation. A joint faculty-trustee committee, chaired by the Reverend Robert Joyce, a UVM graduate and future bishop of the Roman Catholic Diocese of Burlington, found that the professor was no longer a Communist and had never actually been a "real" one, and noted that he had taken the school's loyalty oath and registered for the military draft. The committee voted 5 to 1 to retain Novikoff.

The decision didn't sit well with Emerson or, apparently, many other trustees. Emerson was present when the trustees met next in June. It was the first board meeting he had ever attended. Emerson made a motion that Novikoff be suspended without pay until the professor agreed to answer all of the Senate committee's questions.

The board approved Emerson's motion by a vote of 11 to 5. They gave Novikoff until July 15 to agree to speak.

The *Burlington Daily News* was ecstatic about the decision. In an editorial headlined "Congratulations UVM," the archconservative publisher of the *Daily News,* William Loeb, wrote:

> *This forthright and American type of action is in contrast to the disgusting vacillations and chicken-heartedness of the administration of Harvard University which allowed various members of its faculty to remain at Harvard after they had refused to answer reasonable questions propounded to them by various Congressional committees. . . . Congress and the public have a right to know whether he [Novikoff] is attempting to influence those minds in favor of the Communist conspiracy to destroy this nation.*

Novikoff started getting hate mail, including a death threat. In one of the notes, the writer told him:

> *You have no "constitutional liberty" in trying to undermine a nation that allows rats like you to really amount to something. . . . If you do not get out—you may rest assured your light will go out one of these days and you will be one good Communist—not a live one—you bastard!*

Others were more sympathetic. A group of eighteen Burlington clergy members wrote an open letter to the trustees, urging them to retain Novikoff. The letter also called on trustees to reveal that they had reversed the decision of the Joyce committee, whose recommendation had been kept secret.

Novikoff said years later that he never considered changing his mind, and must have doubted that trustees would change theirs. So he did what any sensible person would do: He dusted off his resume. On June 29, he wrote a letter to one of the world's most famous men, Albert Einstein, seeking help. Novikoff told the famed scientist that he was writing him "because of your deep concern over anti-intellectual activities of Congressional investigating committees." He had reason to believe Einstein would be sympathetic. Just two weeks earlier, Einstein had criticized these types of investigations for instilling "suspicion of all intellectual efforts into the public by dangling before their eyes a danger from without." McCarthy had responded by labeling Einstein an "enemy of America." Novikoff asked Einstein to put in a good word for him at UVM.

Novikoff's supporters pushed for a public hearing, as required under UVM's bylaws. The trustees quickly relented, arranging a meeting of a board of review, which would include faculty members. Novikoff would have one last chance, but not much of one. The university's lawyer set the tone in his rambling accusation against the professor. "He is being discharged because, having knowledge, particular knowledge, knowledge not available to the ordinary communist, even of activities inimical to the security of this country, nevertheless refuses in an investigation of the subversive influence in the educational process to give to a Congressional Committee the benefit of his knowledge."

Exasperated, the professor's lawyer responded that "Dr. Novikoff is charged with the Fifth Amendment." The argument went nowhere. The board of review voted 14 to 8 to recommend that Novikoff be fired. A week later, the trustees made it official, voting almost unanimously to remove Novikoff. The sole dissenter was Rev. Joyce. Novikoff packed his things and left Vermont.

Two years later, he landed a job at the Albert Einstein Medical School, continued his distinguished work as a cancer researcher, and was eventually named to the prestigious American Academy of Sciences.

In 1983, three decades after dismissing him, UVM tried to make amends, honoring Novikoff for his work and presenting him with an honorary degree. Novikoff had already moved past the incident. Novikoff told a reporter: "What I'm asked most of all is do I feel any bitterness, and I don't. I feel that I gained more than I lost. I learned about the understanding and courage of the people who supported me."

THE DEMOCRATIC RESURRECTION

1958

NOBODY WOULD HAVE BLAMED THE DEMOCRATS FOR GIVING UP. After all, in the mid-1950s they were in the midst of a serious losing streak. The last time a Democrat had held a statewide office, the Civil War was still in the future. They had been shut out of office for so long— more than a century—that people could be excused for thinking the prospect of a Democrat actually winning a statewide election was purely theoretical.

But theory became reality in 1958. When the almost unimaginable happened, it happened in a particularly unlikely way. The Democrats finally retook a statewide office with the election of a political novice.

William Meyer and his contribution to the Vermont Democratic Party are almost entirely forgotten today. He was hardly better known when he ran for the U.S. House in 1958.

Meyer was raised in Pennsylvania and moved to Vermont in 1940, at the age of twenty-six, after working in the region as a technician for the Civil Conservation Corps. He settled in southern

Vermont, where he worked as a forester and conservationist. Entering the race for Congress, his only political experience had been a run to represent the town of Rupert in the Vermont House in 1956. He lost.

Meyer was an unpolished public speaker, but his background and his work in the state's forests gave him an easy rapport with rural Vermonters. He had several other things working in his favor. The top of the Democratic ticket featured Frederick Fayette and Bernard Leddy, who were popular and more experienced politicians from Chittenden County. Leddy was running for governor against the GOP candidate Robert Stafford. Fayette was angling for the U.S. Senate seat left vacant by the retirement of Ralph Flanders. Meyer had considered running for that seat, but Fayette had talked him out of it, reportedly making the point that he had a family to support.

Facing Meyer was Harold Arthur, a veteran politician. Arthur had on his resume two years as lieutenant governor and even a brief stint as governor in 1950 after Ernest Gibson Jr. left office to accept a presidential appointment as a federal district judge.

Despite his experience, Arthur was viewed as a weak candidate. He had won the primary, in which he was one of six GOP candidates, with only 30 percent of the vote. That primary was evidence of dissension in the Republican ranks. The party was divided into liberal and conservative wings that didn't particularly get along.

Meyer campaigned as the peace candidate. His stances, which included recognizing Red China, banning nuclear weapons testing, and ending the military draft, were out of step with Democratic leaders both in Vermont and nationally. The country was in the midst of the cold war, and leaders of both major parties weren't interested in appearing soft on anything.

"We cannot continue to befriend dictators at the expense of other peoples," he wrote in one of his campaign brochures. "Nor can we ignore the existence of 'Red' China because we prefer a different form of government."

Meyer worried that fear of war was causing Americans to surrender some of their rights. "We must reclaim our cherished civil liberties and reject those principles and acts which masquerade under the banner of security . . . but lead only to dictatorship."

Vermont Democratic leaders worried that Meyer's outspoken foreign policy positions would cost them any chance of regaining the state's lone U.S. House seat. So the House race featured two candidates that neither party was particularly thrilled about.

Meyer ended up winning the election with 51.5 percent of the vote. He'd been buoyed by endorsements from three nominally Republican daily newspapers in southern Vermont (the *Rutland Herald, Bennington Banner,* and *Brattleboro Reformer*); the support of unions, which contributed $5,200 to the rival candidates—a lot of money in those days; and the voters that Fayette and Leddy attracted to the polls in the Democratic-controlled northwestern corner of the state. Fayette and Leddy ran strong campaigns, but, in the old Democratic tradition, lost.

Walter Smith, chairman of the state Republican Party, reported the unthinkable news to his counterpart in the national party. "We had just one Democratic victory; our congressional seat," Smith wrote, as if it were a regular occurrence. It was, in fact, the Republicans' first statewide election loss ever in Vermont. He blamed the outcome on "a very weak candidate," Harold Arthur, winning the nomination.

Meyer's tenure in Congress lasted a mere two years. Meyer followed through on his campaign promises and spoke out forcefully on peace issues. He worried publicly that Americans were being blinded by fear. "I am tired of having my liberties confined because the faint of heart say it must be done to contain communism," he told the

Vermont Democratic Convention in Rutland in 1960. "I am tired of retreating on all internal fronts because of external threats. I say to you that this course of action not only could eventually destroy democratic government in the United States, but that it would also lose the global struggle for freedom and a better life for all humanity."

Strong words, but not the ones that Vermonters wanted to hear. The state's residents were used to having a fairly liberal delegation in Congress, but for them Meyer's rhetoric was taking things to extremes. Many former supporters abandoned him when he ran for re-election in 1960, and, in typical Democratic fashion, he lost.

Meyer's brief tenure in office helps explain why he isn't remembered as the savior of the Vermont Democratic Party. That honor goes to Phil Hoff, who would win the governor's race in 1962 and, unlike Meyer, manage to hold onto his office.

THE DEMISE OF SMALL-TOWN CLOUT

1965

ON MAY 14, 1965, REPRESENTATIVE FRANK HUTCHINS STOOD before his fellow Vermont House members and cried. Tears of anger, frustration, and sorrow rolled down his cheeks as he denounced a plan he was sure would mean the end of his small town of Stannard and of Vermont as he knew them. Hutchins and representatives of other small towns were about to lose the legislative fight they had been waging. As the sixty-six-year-old farmer spoke, the Legislature was moments away from ending a tradition as old as the state—the tradition of every town sending a representative to the Vermont House.

Federal judges had ordered the Legislature to reapportion the House, to follow the principle of "one man, one vote" rather than "one town, one vote." Before reapportionment, each community had one representative—tiny Stannard and much more populous Burlington, for example, had wielded the same power. After reapportionment, each House member would represent roughly the same number of people.

The retreat from tradition troubled many Vermonters. "When outsiders come into this parlor and tear us to pieces, I regret it," Hutchins said. The reapportionment plan would cut the number of House members from 246 to 150. The change, he warned, would weaken small towns and ensure that many would never again have their own elected representatives. In fact, once the Legislature approved the reapportionment, it would adjourn. After elections that fall, the new slimmed-down House would reconvene, minus many of its smaller-town representatives. In this, his final speech before the Legislature, Hutchins implored his fellow lawmakers: "Don't forget Stannard."

If reapportionment substantially eroded the clout of small towns, it was not like they didn't have ample warning. The one-town, one-vote system in the House had critics from almost the moment it was codified in the Vermont Constitution in 1777.

The framers of the state Constitution had written that they intended to ensure that the "Freemen of this State might enjoy the benefit of election, as equally as may be. . . ." And apparently believing that all Vermont towns would grow at roughly the same pace, they wrote that beginning in 1784, all towns would send just one representative "forever thereafter."

Some Vermonters began pushing for a constitutional change almost immediately. As early as 1785, members of the Council of Censors, responsible for calling constitutional conventions every seven years, proposed setting the number of legislators per county or election district, rather than per town, but the idea died.

The Council of Censors took another shot at reapportionment in 1793. It stuck with the idea of one town, one vote, but wanted to limit that right to towns containing forty or more families. Smaller towns could bond together to elect a representative. The idea, however, was defeated at a constitutional convention, as were subsequent efforts to approve reapportionment.

When reapportionment again failed to gain traction in 1920, supporters angrily complained that "[b]y representative government is not meant the representation of rocks and scenery but the representation of people." The exasperation was understandable. The state's undemocratic method of allocating seats was worsening. Perhaps lawmakers could ignore the fact that in 1849 a House member could represent fewer than 100 constituents or as many as 4,300, but by 1962, the disparities were even more glaring. Stratton, with its 24 residents, had one vote in the House, as did Burlington, with its 35,000 residents. The state's twenty-five largest communities now represented 55 percent of the population but held only 10 percent of the seats in the Legislature.

The disparity shocked some. William Jay Smith, who represented Poultney during the early 1960s, wrote:

> *What we have in Vermont is not just the struggle between rural and urban populations. What we have is not a rural dictatorship, but a rural aristocracy. Being in the Vermont House was for me like a journey back into the 18th century, when one had to own land to vote. . . . The Vermont house is our House of Lords.*

That changed after the U.S. Supreme Court ruled that legislatures had to be apportioned on the basis of population. A federal court in July 1964 ordered the state to reapportion both the House and the Senate by July 1965. So, in the winter of 1965 members of what became known as the "suicide legislature" set to work plotting their own demise. In truth, of course, those from larger communities had a good chance of surviving the process. But many legislators from smaller towns argued hotly against the federal ruling. Representative

Samuel Parsons of Hubbardton worried that if cities dominated the state, then Vermont's character would be destroyed. "Cities aren't healthy minded," he warned. They cause you to "lose sight of what is honorable and dishonorable."

Rep. W. Clark Hutchinson of Rochester so opposed reapportionment that he vowed to chain himself to his House desk if the measure passed. "We know that forced reapportionment is loss of self-government, and we intend to fight, and we intend to vote against it now and forever," he declared. The small towns that had always ruled Vermont were not going down without a fight.

Despite the emotions, the vote wasn't even close. Lawmakers approved the reapportionment, 163 to 62. Many lawmakers approved the plan that would cost them their seats. And no legislator chained himself to his desk.

Reapportionment realigned power in the state, as it was supposed to, shifting a greater proportion of seats to where more people lived—the cities.

The changes also helped create a true two-party system. Democrats, long in the minority, began to pick up seats and eventually took over the House from the Republicans, who had relied on the many seats they had held in small, rural, and reliably conservative towns. In reducing the number of rural representatives, reapportionment also had the unintended consequence of reducing the numbers of farmers in the Legislature.

One farmer to leave the House was Frank Hutchins of Stannard. Hutchins had warned that reapportionment would be the undoing of small towns in Vermont. He may have been right. And so far he was definitely right about one other thing: Stannard has yet to send another representative to the Statehouse.

TO DOME OR NOT TO DOME

1980

WHEN R. BUCKMINSTER FULLER WALKED TO THE MICROPHONE, the crowd of nearly one thousand people had a pretty good idea what he would say. But they came to listen anyway.

Fuller was the world's leading, or at least most famous, futuristic architect and inventor—he preferred to call himself a "comprehensive, anticipatory design scientist" or, more simply, a "comprehensivist." The eighty-four-year-old Fuller was the keynote speaker at the International Dome Symposium hosted by St. Michael's College in March 1980. He knew a thing or two about domes, having invented the geodesic dome, a metal structure enveloped by a thin membrane that offered a sturdy and comparatively inexpensive way to cover large areas, like industrial storage facilities, sports fields, or, say, the city of Winooski.

Fuller had proven that the first two applications worked; he was in Vermont to argue that the third application was equally viable. Think of it as a super Superdome. The suggestion that Winooski could be domed had been discussed seriously at city council meetings, in the newspapers, and in living rooms. Opinion divided over whether it was an innovative proposal or merely an insane idea.

But the time seemed ripe for unconventional thinking. The year was 1980 and the United States was suffering from high energy prices. A dome over Winooski, supporters argued, was a reasonable response, since, they argued, it could cut the city's heating costs by 90 percent.

To some, Fuller's presence at the conference gave the sense that Winooski was on the cutting edge. To others, however, it suggested the city had gone *over* that edge. Although Fuller will always be remembered for his geodesic domes, he also dreamt up a flying car, a prefab bathroom unit (which came complete with preinstalled toilet, tub, and sink), and a giant domed Japanese island city that could hold 1 million people and float in Tokyo Bay. As the writer of a magazine profile of the inventor once wrote, "Fuller's schemes often had the hallucinatory quality associated with science fiction (or mental hospitals)."

During his speech in Winooski, Fuller didn't speak to the specifics of doming the city. Instead, in a wide-ranging talk citing everything from the discovery by nineteenth-century British political economist Thomas Malthus that the world's population was growing faster than our ability to support life to the recent crossing of the English Channel by the ultralightweight, human-power aircraft *The Gossamer Condor,* Fuller said the world needed to learn to do more with less.

For all the public interest in Fuller, the Winooski dome wasn't his idea. Winooski's community development director, Mark Tigan, was its leading proponent, though he credited an official with the U.S. Department of Housing and Urban Development agency (HUD) with originating the idea.

"It would be the ultimate in Yankee ingenuity," Tigan told *Time* magazine in December 1979. Tigan explained that the city was considering one-dome and two-dome options. If one dome were built, it would be large enough to cover 850 acres. If two were built, a twenty-five-acre dome would cover the downtown core and a fifty-acre dome would cover the city's industrial park. Also to be determined, Tigan said, was whether a dome could be retracted in good weather.

Some local residents united around the issue, forming the Golden Onion Dome Club. The "onion" part of the name referred to the city's name (Winooski means wild onion in Abenaki), not the shape of the dome, which in sketches looked more like a giant contact lens. Club members created bumper stickers, T-shirts, even a song, supporting the unusual proposal. It's unclear whether they thought a dome was a good idea or just a funny one.

(The words to the song "Dome Over Winooski" were: "Dome over Winooski, / Not far from the lake; / Transparent and plastic, / Still real and not fake.")

Not surprisingly, people raised concerns about the dome. Beyond questioning its feasibility and its potential to interfere with the flight path of the nearby Burlington airport, some residents said they didn't want to be isolated from the natural world. Others had a more mundane worry: Who would wash the dome's windows? One answer: members of the city road crew who would no longer have to plow the streets.

Some people suggested that in addition to reducing Winooski's energy consumption, a dome could make Winooski a tourist attraction. One local writer quipped that Winooski might become a popular winter vacation alternative to Florida.

To answer these and other questions, the city's Community Development Committee voted 3 to 2 to apply for a $55,000 HUD grant to commission a feasibility study.

"A lot of people think it's a bizarre idea until you sit them down and explain it to them," Tigan told a United Press International reporter. "Once people listen, we haven't heard a single negative person."

Shoji Sadao, Fuller's partner in his New York City architecture firm, also said a city-size dome might be possible. In fact, Fuller and Sadao had proposed a two-mile-diameter dome for the north end of Manhattan. "Maybe we're getting out of the realm where this is just a pipe dream or visionary, and slowly getting into the realm of the practical," Sadao told *Time*.

Toward the end of his Winooski speech, Fuller called on people to think beyond the conventional. While working for the federal government as a scientist during World War II, Fuller said, he had discovered that he could get automobile engines to run more efficiently and with fewer emissions by fueling them with alcohol instead of gasoline. But, he said, word of his experiments never got out. He smelled a conspiracy. "Nobody has any idea how incredibly powerful oil money really is," Fuller said. "It is controlling advertising, and newspapers cannot publish unless they have advertising."

Still, he saw reason for hope. Fuller said he had been born into a world that was 95 percent illiterate. By 1980, he said, most people could read and an informed populace could make good decisions.

"Humanity is now literate, and it is a wonderful thing that your community, Winooski, has stood up and said let's make some sense," he said. "I couldn't be more encouraged by what has happened here."

But, you might have noticed, Winooski isn't domed today. After the dome conference, the Department of Housing and Urban Development rejected the city's request for money to study the proposal, and the idea died.

Before the proposal was rejected, however, Mark Tigan said he viewed the dome idea as a long-term solution, not a quick fix. A dome, he said, has "never been examined on this scale before. It's time to look at some of these things that people think are flaky but might be turning to in the next ten or fifteen years."

THE MEN OF MAPLE CORNER

2001

Stanley Fitch was not your typical nude model. He was a seventy-eight-year-old retired dairy farmer when international fame, and exposure, briefly found him and a dozen other men from his town.

Fitch got his big modeling break when he was asked to pose for a calendar. Some of his neighbors had decided on an offbeat way to raise money for the Maple Corner Community Center building in Calais. The century-old building, which had started life as headquarters for the local Grange, needed repairs to comply with fire codes and septic regulations.

Fitch agreed right away to drop everything to help his community. "I figured, at my age, what difference does it make?" he said. Besides, organizers were only planning to print five hundred copies. Who was going to see it, really?

Organizers hoped the calendar might raise more money than more traditional fund-raisers. With a bake sale, Fitch told the local newspaper, "You end up with 150 bucks or something, when you need something like $29,000. We had to try something new."

But Fitch, and the project's organizers, got more than they'd bargained for. Before long, Fitch and others in this small community were talking to more than just the local paper. The Associated Press sent out on the news wire a photograph taken of a photo shoot for the calendar. Newspapers around the country ran the photo. *USA Today* wrote a story. Regional newspapers and television stations produced their own reports. A Japanese radio station organized a live interview. Then a satellite truck for NBC's *Today* pulled up next to the community center.

It was all a bit surreal for the people of Maple Corner, a neighborhood of about a dozen homes in Calais. The project had taken on a life of its own.

The idea had grown out of a conversation between a few residents who were brainstorming fund-raising ideas. Cornelia Emlen had recently seen the movie *The Full Monty,* in which a group of unemployed male steel workers make money by putting on a nude revue. Emlen also knew about the remarkably successful fund-raising calendar created by The Ladies of Rylstone, England, who had posed discretely for photographs in their domestic environments.

Emlen thought Maple Corner could replicate that calendar's success, albeit on a smaller scale, by using local men for models. "We have all these guys who aren't you-crane-your-neck-to-look-at-them kind of guys, but they are very attractive, because they are very nice," Emlen explained. She began her recruitment drive at the community's annual corn roast. After clearing it with Stanley Fitch's wife, she asked the well-liked farmer to pose. Then she used Fitch's name as a recruitment tool. Some quickly signed up; others asked Emlen how much they needed to donate *not* to appear in the calendar.

In the end, thirteen men, ranging in age from thirty to seventy-eight, volunteered. To deal with the slight surplus, brothers J.C. and Matt Myers shared the month of November.

The production budget was tight. Local photographer Craig Line volunteered to shoot the photos; professional designers Heather Pelham and Thom Milke volunteered to create the calendar. To pay for printing, organizers sold advance copies.

The name was originally going to be "The Full Vermonty." Twentieth Century Fox, the U.S. distributor for the *The Full Monty,* agreed to license the name, but only if the calendars weren't sold outside of Calais. With nothing like a legal budget, calendar organizers decided they'd rather switch than fight. Thus was born "The Men of Maple Corner." In truth, the models were drawn from "Greater Maple Corner," but even that geographical description takes in only a few dozen more houses.

The models came from all walks of life and were photographed in personal, if discrete, poses. "Mr. July," David Schutz, the curator of the nearby Vermont Statehouse and an occasional actor, posed wearing the major general's hat used in a recent local production of *Pirates of Penzance,* with small Jolly Roger and Union Jack flags providing him some modesty. "Mr. April," Don Heise, a fishing guide, posed in a rowboat, partly screened by the mounted fish he is holding. And Fitch, aka "Mr. March," posed pouring maple sap from a bucket in his maple sugarhouse.

The timing was right. The terrorist attacks of 9/11 had just occurred and so much of what was filling the news was frightening. At first, organizers fretted that perhaps their lighthearted calendar was inappropriate for the times, but they decided that humor was a remedy for sorrow. It was what people wanted. After that first AP photo hit the wire, the news media couldn't get enough.

That helps explain why a team from *Today* arranged to do a live remote from Maple Corner. Before the broadcast, folks with NBC had suggested that the calendar organizers might want to have a toll-free number that could be given out on the air. During the broadcast, one of the models, Chris Miller ("Mr. February") joked that he objected to the interjection of commercialism into the process. "You've turned us from supermodels to shameless hucksters in one day," he said.

Fortunately, calendar organizers had taken the advice about the toll-free number seriously, but they soon realized that all toll-free phone services aren't the same. "We didn't realize how many people were going to call," said Emlen. The calls overwhelmed the service. Orders crashed the calendar Web site. Vermont bookstores kept demanding more copies; they couldn't keep them in stock.

The men of Maple Corner became minor celebrities. A book signing in Burlington drew a crowd that stretched down the block. They were invited to send a representative to the television game show *To Tell the Truth*. The men drew lots, and Matt Myers won the honor of appearing.

A blizzard of mail orders arrived, leaving drifts several feet high some days. When it was all done, community members had printed not five hundred calendars but forty thousand. And, taking in $500,000, they shot well past their fund-raising goal of $30,000. Needless to say, the community center got its repairs and now has a sizeable endowment.

Many calendar orders came in with personal notes to the models, often complimenting them on their looks and/or their courage. One of the most fitting tributes came from a woman who identified herself as Sally from Sioux City, South Dakota. She wrote, "It took the 'Men of Maple Corner' to make America laugh again."

BIBLIOGRAPHY

Acknowledgments

This book grew out of a weekly column I began writing in 2002 for *Vermont Sunday Magazine,* which is published by the *Rutland Herald* and *Barre-Montpelier Times Argus* newspapers. Early versions of many of the stories in this book first saw life in the papers' pages. It has been my great good fortune that many Vermonters cared enough about the state's past to make reading the column a regular part of their Sunday routine.

My principal editor for the original columns was Dirk Van Susteren, who was kind enough not to laugh at the idea that history could be newsworthy, and that a history column could be written in a way that was compelling and relevant to contemporary readers.

Dirk believed in the column and for years encouraged me to have a collection of them published as a book. Fortunately, Megan Hiller, an editor for Globe Pequot called, looking for just such a book.

Before I researched and wrote these stories, I needed to know each topic was worth pursuing. For this I relied on a variety of sources. I was fortunate that an excellent survey of Vermont history appeared shortly before I began this project. *Freedom and Unity,* by Michael Sherman, Gene Sessions, and P. Jeffrey Potash, was published in 2004 by the Vermont Historical Society, and was invaluable to me in providing context for the periods about which I was writing.

I also relied heavily for story ideas on Vermont's historians. I can't even begin to guess how many story ideas grew out of conversations with Marjorie Strong and Paul Carnahan, librarians at the Vermont Historical Society, and with Vermont State Archivist Gregory Sanford. John Duffy, professor emeritus of English and humanities from Johnson State College, patiently shared his scholarship on eighteenth-century Vermont when I couldn't find books that would surrender the answers.

In writing these essays, I often needed help weeding out extraneous details to make the stories compelling for the general reader. In addition to Dirk Van Susteren, three other people have been particularly helpful: Anne Galloway and Ruth Hare, who have at different times taken on Dirk's role at the paper, and my wife, Susan Clark, who was patient in listening to my travails and wise in offering solutions.

I've also been lucky that while I've been immersing myself in the past, my son, Harrison, has kept me happily rooted in the present.

A Killing Winter for the French, 1666–1667

Coolidge, Guy. *The French Occupation of the Champlain Valley from 1609–1759.* Mamaroneck, N.Y.: Harbor Hill Books, 1989.

Crockett, Walter Hill. *A History of Lake Champlain: A Record of Three Centuries, 1609–1909.* Burlington, Vt.: H. J. Shanley & Co., 1909.

Hill, Ralph Nading. *Lake Champlain: Key to Liberty.* Woodstock, Vt.: The Countryman Press, 1976.

Kerlidou, Joseph, Joseph N. Couture, and Maurice U. Boucher. *St. Anne's Shrine, Isle La Motte, Vt.; on the Shores of Beautiful Lake Champlain.* Isle La Motte, Vt.: The Shrine, 1979.

The Westminster Massacre, 1775

French, J. M., MD. "The Westminster Massacre." *New England Monthly,* November 1891.

Hall, Benjamin Homer. "History of Eastern Vermont, From Its Earliest Settlement to the Close of the Eighteenth Century." Troy, N.Y.: Educator's International Press, 2001. Facsimile reproduction. Original published New York: D. Appleton & Co., 1858.

Latham, Leon D. "First Blood of the Revolution—Where?" *The Vermonter,* January 1937.

Van de Water, Frederic F. *The Reluctant Republic: Vermont 1724–1791.* Taftsville, Vt.: The Countryman Press. 1974.

The Road from Nowhere to Nowhere, 1776

Baldwin, Frederick W. "The Hazen Military Road." *The Vermonter,* November 1906.

Brinton, Crane. "The Hazen Road: Canada Wasn't Invaded After All from This 175-Year Old Military Highway, But It Served Vermont a Better Way." *Vermont Life,* Spring 1955.

McCorison, Marcus A. *The Bayley-Hazen Military Road.* Norwich, Vt.: The Pine Tree Press, 1959.

The Royalton Raid, 1780

Barrows, Alice C. "The Royalton Indian Raid, for Motorists." *The Vermonter,* October 1936.

Calloway, Colin G. "The Conquest of Vermont: Vermont's Indian Troubles in Context." *Vermont History,* Summer 1984.

———. *The Western Abenaki of Vermont, 1600–1800: War, Migration and Survival of an Indian People.* Norman: University of Oklahoma Press, 1990.

Prince, John Conger. "The Burning of Royalton, Vermont by Indians, in 1780." *The Vermonter,* October 1930.

The Cow Wars, 1782

Bellesiles, Michael A. *Revolutionary Outlaws: Ethan Allen and the Struggle for Independence on the Early American Frontier.* Charlottesville and London: University Press of Virginia, 1995.

Jellison, Charles A. *Ethan Allen: Frontier Rebel.* Syracuse, N.Y.: Syracuse University Press, 1969.

The Visit of Two Founders, 1791

Bellico, Russell P. *Chronicles of Lake Champlain: Journeys in War and Peace.* Fleischmanns, N.Y.: Purple Mountain Press, 1999.

Hill, Ralph Nading. *Lake Champlain: Key to Liberty.* Woodstock, Vt.: The Countryman Press, 1976.

Maguire, J. Robert, ed. *The Tour to the Northern Lakes of James Madison & Thomas Jefferson, May–June 1791.* Ticonderoga, N.Y.: Fort Ticonderoga, 1995.

Randall, Willard Sterne. "Thomas Jefferson Takes a Vacation." *American Heritage,* July/August 1996.

The Trial of Matthew Lyon, 1799

Austin, Aleine. Matthew Lyon, "New Man" of the Democratic
Revolution, 1749–1822. University Park: Pennsylvania State
University Press, 1981.

Montagno, George, L. "Federalist Retaliation: The Sedition Trial
of Matthew Lyon." Vermont History, January 1958.

The Slave Trial, 1802

Conlin, Katherine E. "Dinah, and the Slave Question in Vermont."
Vermont History, October 1953.

Fairbanks, Henry. "Slavery and the Vermont Clergy." *Vermont
History,* October 1959.

Tyler, Royal. "Reports of Cases Argued and Determined in the
Supreme Court of Judicature of the State of Vermont." New
York: I. Riley, 1809–1810.

White, Rev. Pliny H. "Theopilus Harrington: A Paper read
before the Vermont Historical Society, at a Special Meeting of
Rutland, 20th August, 1868." Published in the *Rutland Herald,*
December 15, 1868.

The *Black Snake* Affair, 1808

Crockett, Walter H. *Vermont: The Green Mountain State.* New
York: The Century History Co., 1921.

Duffy, John J. "Broadsides Illustrations of the Jeffersonian-
Federalist Conflict in Vermont, 1809–1816." *Vermont History,*
Fall 1981.

Muller, H. N. "Smuggling into Canada: How the Champlain Valley Defied Jeffferson's Embargo." *Vermont History,* Winter 1970.

"To the People of Vermont." Broadside, published 1808.

The Year without a Summer, 1816

Bassett, T. D. Seymour. "The Cold Summer of 1816 in Vermont: Fact and Folklore." *New England Galaxy,* Summer 1973.

———. "The Gods of the Hills: Piety and Society in Nineteenth-Century Vermont." Montpelier: Vermont Historical Society, 2000.

Hard, Walter R. Jr., and Janet C. Greene, eds. *Mischief in the Mountains.* Montpelier: *Vermont Life* magazine, 1970.

Ludlum, David McWilliams. *The Vermont Weather Book.* Montpelier: The Vermont Historical Society, 1985.

The *Phoenix* Steamboat Disaster, 1819

Davison, Rebecca, ed. "The *Phoenix* Project: A Report from the Champlain Maritime Society with Funds from the Vermont Division for Historic Preservation." Burlington: Vermont Maritime Society, 1981.

Hill, Ralph Nading. *Lake Champlain: Key to Liberty.* Woodstock, Vt.: The Countryman Press, 1976.

Ross, Ogden. *Steamboats of Lake Champlain, 1809 to 1930.* Quechee: Vermont Heritage Press, 1997.

The Boorn "Murder" Mystery, 1819

An anonymous member of the Massachusetts Bar. *Mysteries of Crime as Shown in Remarkable Capital Trials.* Boston: Samuel Walker & Co., 1870.

Hard, Walter R. Jr., and Janet C. Greene, eds. *Mischief in the Mountains.* Montpelier: *Vermont Life* magazine, 1970.

McFarland, Gerald W. *The "Counterfeit" Man: The True Story of the Boorn-Colvin Murder Case.* New York: Pantheon Books, 1990.

The Millerite Miscalculation, 1844

Davis, Allen F. "The Girl He Left Behind: The Letters of Harriet Hutchinson Salisbury." *Vermont History,* January 1965.

Nichols, Francis D. *The Midnight Cry: A Defense of William Miller and the Millerites.* Washington, D.C.: Review and Herald Publishing Association, 1945.

Sears, Clara Endicott. *Days of Delusion.* Boston: Houghton Mifflin Co., 1924.

Silitch, Clarissa. *Mad and Magnificent Yankees.* Dublin, N.H.: Yankee Books, 1973.

The Phineas Gage Accident, 1848

Blakeslee, Sandra. "Old Accident Points to Brain's Moral Center." *The New York Times,* May 24, 1994.

Fleischman, John. "Like a Hole in the Head: The Tale of a Famous and Bizarre Medical Miracle." *Yankee,* October 1999.

Harlow, John M., MD. *Recovery from the Passage of an Iron Bar Through the Head.* Boston: David Clapp & Son, 1869.

Harlow, John M., to Harold Rugg, September 14, 1904. Collection of the Vermont Historical Society.

MacMillan, Malcolm. *An Odd Kind of Fame: Stories of Phineas Gage.* Cambridge: Massachusetts Institute of Technology Press, 2000.

———. "A Wonderful Journey Through the Skull and Brains: The Travels of Mr. Gage's Tamping Iron." *Brain and Cognition,* January 1986.

A Counterfeiting Scheme, 1850

Ormsbee, Thomas Hamilton. "Christian Meadows, Engraver and Counterfeiter." *American Collector,* January 1945.

———. *A Storehouse of Antiques.* New York: Robert M. McBride & Co., 1947.

Roberts, Gwilym. "Elijah Remington, The Castleton Counterfeiter." *Vermont History,* Vol. 34, 1966.

Scott, Kenneth. "Counterfeiting in Early Vermont." *Vermont History,* Vol. 22, 1965.

Webster, Daniel, to Vermont governor Charles Williams, October 2, 1857. Collection of the Vermont Historical Society.

A Breakthrough for Women, 1852

Bassett, T. D. Seymour, "The 1870 Campaign for Woman Suffrage in Vermont." *Vermont Quarterly,* April 1946.

————. *The Growing Edge: Vermont Villages, 1840–1880.* Montpelier: Vermont Historical Society, 1992.

Blackwell, Marilyn Schultz. Interview, November 2002.

Kunin, Madeleine May. "Clarina Howard Nichols: Green Mountain Suffragette." *Vermont Life,* Winter 1973.

Nichols, Clarina I. Howard. "Reminiscences by Clarina I. Howard Nichols" in *History of Woman Suffrage,* edited by Elizabeth Cady Stanton, Susan B. Anthony, and Matilda Josyln Gage. Rochester, N.Y.: Charles Mann, 1889.

The St. Albans Raid, 1864

Horan, James D. *Confederate Agent: A Discovery in History.* New York: Crown Publishing, Inc., 1954.

St. Albans Messenger, various articles from October 19–25, 1864.

Wilson, Dennis K. *Justice Under Pressure: The Saint Albans Raid and Its Aftermath.* Lanham, Md.; London, New York: University Press of America, 1992.

The Fenian Invasion, 1866

Calkin, Homer. "St. Albans in Reverse: The Fenian Raid of 1866." *Vermont History,* January 1967.

MacDonald, John A. *Troublous Times in Canada, A History of the Fenian Raids of 1866 and 1870.* Toronto: W. S. Johnson & Co., 1910.

Missisquoi County Historical Society. *The Fenian Raids, 1866–1870.* Stanbridge East, Quebec: Missisquoi County Historical Society, 1967.

Ó Broin, León. *Fenian Fever: An Anglo-American Dilemma.* New York: New York University Press, 1971.

Rowsome, Frank Jr., and Joan Steen. "The Fenian Raid." *Vermont Life,* Summer 1961.

Senior, Hereward. *The Last Invasion of Canada: The Fenian Raids, 1866–1870.* Toronto, Oxford: Dundurn Press, 1991.

Taylor, John M. "Fenian Raids Against Canada." *American History Illustrated,* August 1978.

Walker, Mabel Gregory. *The Fenian Movement.* Colorado Springs, Colo.: R. Myles, 1969.

The Burlington Winter Carnival, 1886

Beattie, Betsy. "The Queen City Celebrates Winter: The Burlington Coasting Club and the Burlington Carnival of Winter Sports, 1886–1887." *Vermont History,* Winter 1984.

The West Hartford Train Wreck, 1887

Griswold, Wesley S. "Disaster at White River Train Bridge." *Vermont Life,* Winter 1969.

———. *Train Wreck.* Brattleboro: Stephen Greene Press, 1969.

McCartney, Charlotte. "Hartford Railroad Disaster." *Rural Vermonter,* Spring 1963.

Teddy Learns McKinley's Been Shot, 1901

Forbes, C. S. "President Roosevelt." *The Vermonter,* November 1901.

Hill, Ralph Nading. "Days of Glory at Lt. Gov. Nelson Fisk's Isle La Motte Showplace and Two Presidential Visits Are Recalled by Ralph Nading Hill." *Vermont Life,* Summer 1966.

The Jailing of a Minister, 1917

Sessions, Gene. "Espionage in Windsor: Clarence H. Waldron and Patriotism in World War I." *Vermont History,* Summer 1993.

The Famous Ice Floe Scene, 1920

Gish, Lillian. Interview by Ethan Hubbard in 1972.

Gordon, Rachel. Handwritten notes of her recollections. Collection of the Vermont Historical Society.

"Lillian Gish Says She Was More Hardy in the Sub-Zero Winter Weather in Vermont than the Dartmouth College Students Who Watched Her Film-Making from the Banks of the White River in 1920." *Vermont History News and Notes,* February 1971.

Maurice, Maggie. "The 112-Pound Dynamo Who Never Uses a Double." *Burlington Free Press,* October 29, 1971.

Maurice, Maggie, and Walter Hubbard. "Way Down East." *Vermont Life,* Spring 1973.

Coolidge's Summer White House, 1924

Various newspaper articles from the *Rutland Daily Herald* and the *Vermont Standard* (of Woodstock) during the period of August 16–29, 1924.

The Great Flood, 1927

Chadwick, Harold H. "Flood: In the Days Before Flood Protection, a Quarter Century Ago, Vermonters Proved Their Mettle in the Face of Disaster." *Vermont Life,* Autumn 1952.

Johnson, Luther B. *Vermont in Floodtime.* Randolph: Roy L. Johnson Company, 1927.

Plaisted, Edgell R. "Going Thro Hell and High Water." *The Vermonter,* December 1927.

Seidman, Sarah, and Patricia Wiley. *Middlesex in the Making: History and Memories of a Small Vermont Town.* Middlesex, Vt.: Middlesex Historical Society, 2006.

The Defeat of the Green Mountain Parkway, 1935

Bancroft, Ernest H. "Why People Should Favor the Green Mountain Parkway" in *Vermont Voices, 1609 to 1990: A Documentary History of the Green Mountain State,* ed. J. Kevin Graffagnino. Montpelier: Vermont Historical Society, 1999.

Goldman, Hal. "James Taylor's Progressive Vision: The Green Mountain Parkway." *Vermont History,* Summer 1995.

"No Green Mountain Hot-Dogs: Vermonters, Through Town
Meetings, Make Sure Barkers Will Not Cry in Their Unspoiled
Wilderness by Vetoing Federal Parkway." *The Literary Digest,*
March 14, 1936.

Silverstein, Hannah. "No Parking: Vermont Rejects the Green
Mountain Parkway." *Vermont History,* Summer 1995.

The Camel's Hump Crash, 1944

Lindner, Brian. Interview, January 2004.

———. "The History of the Camel's Hump Bomber Crash," self-
published manuscript, 1978.

The Novikoff Firing, 1953

Holmes, David R. *Stalking the Academic Communist: Intellectual
Freedom and the Firing of Alex Novikoff.* Hanover, N.H.:
University Press of New England, 1989.

Polumbaum, Judy. "UVM Professors Have Been Stung: Academic
World Vulnerable to Political Forces." *Rutland Herald,* March
26, 1979.

The Democratic Resurrection, 1958

Hand, Samuel B. *The Star that Set: The Vermont Republican Party,
1854–1974.* Lanham, Md.; London, New York: Lexington
Books, 2002.

Jacobson, Peter, and Earl Medlinsky. "The Meyer Campaign." *New
University Thought,* Spring 1961.

The Demise of Small-Town Clout, 1965

Hand, Samuel B. *The Star that Set: The Vermont Republican Party, 1854–1974.* Lanham, Md.; London, New York: Lexington Books, 2002.

Nuquist, Andrew E., and Edith W. Nuquist. *Vermont State Government and Administration: An Historical and Descriptive Study of the Living Past.* Burlington: Government Research Center, University of Vermont, 1966.

Terry, Stephen C. " 'One Person, One Vote': The Impact of Reapportionment on Vermont, 1777–1992." *Vermont History,* Spring 1993.

To Dome or Not To Dome, 1980

Burlington Free Press, various newspaper articles during the period of November 1979 through March 1980.

"A Dome for Winooski? A Far-Out Scheme Could Reduce the City's Heating Bills." *Time,* December, 10, 1979.

Proceedings: International Dome Symposium. Saint Michael's College, Winooski, Vt., March 26–27, 1980.

The Men of Maple Corner, 2001

Various newspaper articles by David W. Smith and Stephen Mills of the *Barre-Montpelier Times Argus* and Anne Wallace Allen of the Associated Press during the period of October 2001 through February 2002.

Calta, Marialisa. "Maple Corner's Men Go Global." *Vermont Life,* Spring 2002.

Emlen, Cornelia, and Marialisa Calta. Interviews, November 2008.

INDEX

ABOUT THE AUTHOR

Mark Bushnell worked for a dozen years as an editor for Vermont newspapers. Realizing that writers have move fun than editors, he began freelancing and since 2002 has written a weekly column about Vermont history, called "Life in the Past Lane," for the *Rutland Herald* and *Barre-Montpelier Times Argus*. He is the author of *Discover Vermont! The Vermont Life Guide to Exploring Our Rural Landscape* and contributed a chapter to a biography of Howard Dean. He lives in Middlesex, Vermont, with his wife, Susan Clark, and son, Harrison.